The Tragedy of Richard the Third

By Edward de Vere

Art:
Portrait of Edward de Vere
17th Earl of Oxford (1550-1604)

This edition produced by
Verus Publishing

www.verusbooks.com

Copyright 2019 Verus Publishing
This book, with the exception of the text of the play itself, remains the copyrighted property of the publisher and may not be duplicated or redistributed in whole or in part without express permission.

ISBN: 978-1-951267-25-4
Imprint / Publisher: Verus Publishing

The Author

Edward de Vere, 17th Earl of Oxford

Biography and Bibliography
After the Play

A Preverse

Drone on ye learned scholars of the day
As to with whom the words ahead the credit lay.
For our part though can be no further doubt
That the author of these words has been found out
To be a person lordly and refined
On whom the light of wit so boldly shined
That to keep this wit from tearing in the fray
He gave another, lesser wit his say.

Now let the least of wits
That writes these paltry lines
Yield to him whose peerless name
Should be with reverence spake.
Let this name be not of history's misassigns
Whose pen and verse have made the earth to shake.

The Tragedy of Richard the Third

By Edward de Vere

The Main Characters

House of York
King Edward IV – King of England
Richard, Duke of Gloucester – Edward IV's brother; later King Richard III
George, Duke of Clarence – Edward IV's brother
Duchess of York – Edward, Richard and George's mother
Edward, Prince of Wales – Edward IV's eldest son; later King Edward V (never crowned)
Richard, Duke of York – Edward IV's son
Boy – George's son
Girl – George's daughter

House of Lancaster
Queen Margaret – widow of King Henry VI
Ghost of King Henry VI

Ghost of Edward of Westminster, Prince of Wales – Henry VI's son
Lady Anne Neville – widow of Edward of Westminster; later wife of King Richard III
Tressel and Berkeley – Lady Anne's attendants (non-speaking roles)

Woodville family
Queen Elizabeth – wife of King Edward IV
Earl Rivers – Elizabeth's brother
Marquis of Dorset – Elizabeth's son (from a previous marriage)
Lord Richard Grey – Elizabeth's son (from a previous marriage)
Sir Thomas Vaughan – ally of Rivers and Grey

Richard III's group
Duke of Buckingham
Sir William Catesby
Duke of Norfolk
Earl of Surrey – Norfolk's son
Sir Richard Ratcliffe
Sir James Tyrrell – assassin
Lord Love
Two Murderers
Richard's page

(Continued)

Earl of Richmond's group

Henry Tudor, Earl of Richmond – Henry VI's nephew; later King Henry VII

Lord Stanley, Earl of Derby – Richmond's stepfather

Earl of Oxford

Sir Walter Herbert

Sir James Blunt

Sir William Brandon – Richmond's standard-bearer (non-speaking role)

Clergy

Archbishop of Canterbury

Archbishop of York

Bishop of Ely

Sir Christopher – chaplain of Stanley's household

John – priest

Other characters

Lord Hastings – Lord Chamberlain under Edward IV

Sir Robert Brackenbury – Lieutenant of the Tower

Lord Mayor of London

Scrivener

Keeper of the Tower

Three Citizens
Hastings
Sheriff of Wiltshire

Ghosts... of Clarence, Rivers, Grey, Vaughan, Edward (Prince of Wales), Richard (Duke of York), Hastings, Lady Anne and Buckingham

Lords, Messengers, Soldiers etc.

And now, the Play...

ACT I

SCENE I.
London. A street.

Enter GLOUCESTER, solus

GLOUCESTER
  Now is the winter of our discontent
  Made glorious summer by this sun of York;
  And all the clouds that lour'd upon our house
  In the deep bosom of the ocean buried.
  Now are our brows bound with victorious wreaths;
  Our bruised arms hung up for monuments;
  Our stern alarums changed to merry meetings,
  Our dreadful marches to delightful measures.
  Grim-visaged war hath smooth'd his wrinkled front;
  And now, instead of mounting barbed steeds
  To fright the souls of fearful adversaries,
  He capers nimbly in a lady's chamber
  To the lascivious pleasing of a lute.
  But I, that am not shaped for sportive tricks,
  Nor made to court an amorous looking-glass;
  I, that am rudely stamp'd, and want love's majesty
  To strut before a wanton ambling nymph;
  I, that am curtail'd of this fair proportion,
  Cheated of feature by dissembling nature,
  Deformed, unfinish'd, sent before my time
  Into this breathing world, scarce half made up,
  And that so lamely and unfashionable
  That dogs bark at me as I halt by them;
  Why, I, in this weak piping time of peace,
  Have no delight to pass away the time,

The Tragedy of Richard the Third— Act I

Unless to spy my shadow in the sun
And descant on mine own deformity:
And therefore, since I cannot prove a lover,
To entertain these fair well-spoken days,
I am determined to prove a villain
And hate the idle pleasures of these days.
Plots have I laid, inductions dangerous,
By drunken prophecies, libels and dreams,
To set my brother Clarence and the king
In deadly hate the one against the other:
And if King Edward be as true and just
As I am subtle, false and treacherous,
This day should Clarence closely be mew'd up,
About a prophecy, which says that 'G'
Of Edward's heirs the murderer shall be.
Dive, thoughts, down to my soul: here
Clarence comes.

Enter CLARENCE, guarded, and BRAKENBURY

Brother, good day; what means this armed guard
That waits upon your grace?
CLARENCE
  His majesty
  Tendering my person's safety, hath appointed
  This conduct to convey me to the Tower.
GLOUCESTER
  Upon what cause?
CLARENCE
  Because my name is George.
GLOUCESTER
  Alack, my lord, that fault is none of yours;
  He should, for that, commit your godfathers:
  O, belike his majesty hath some intent
  That you shall be new-christen'd in the Tower.

The Tragedy of Richard the Third— Act I

But what's the matter, Clarence? may I know?
CLARENCE
Yea, Richard, when I know; for I protest
As yet I do not: but, as I can learn,
He hearkens after prophecies and dreams;
And from the cross-row plucks the letter G.
And says a wizard told him that by G
His issue disinherited should be;
And, for my name of George begins with G,
It follows in his thought that I am he.
These, as I learn, and such like toys as these
Have moved his highness to commit me now.
GLOUCESTER
Why, this it is, when men are ruled by women:
'Tis not the king that sends you to the Tower:
My Lady Grey his wife, Clarence, 'tis she
That tempers him to this extremity.
Was it not she and that good man of worship,
Anthony Woodville, her brother there,
That made him send Lord Hastings to the Tower,
From whence this present day he is deliver'd?
We are not safe, Clarence; we are not safe.
CLARENCE
By heaven, I think there's no man is secure
But the queen's kindred and night-walking heralds
That trudge betwixt the king and Mistress Shore.
Heard ye not what an humble suppliant
Lord hastings was to her for his delivery?
GLOUCESTER
Humbly complaining to her deity
Got my lord chamberlain his liberty.
I'll tell you what; I think it is our way,
If we will keep in favour with the king,
To be her men and wear her livery:

The Tragedy of Richard the Third— Act I

    The jealous o'erworn widow and herself,
    Since that our brother dubb'd them gentlewomen.
    Are mighty gossips in this monarchy.
BRAKENBURY
    I beseech your graces both to pardon me;
    His majesty hath straitly given in charge
    That no man shall have private conference,
    Of what degree soever, with his brother.
GLOUCESTER
    Even so; an't please your worship, Brakenbury,
    You may partake of any thing we say:
    We speak no treason, man: we say the king
    Is wise and virtuous, and his noble queen
    Well struck in years, fair, and not jealous;
    We say that Shore's wife hath a pretty foot,
    A cherry lip, a bonny eye, a passing pleasing tongue;
    And that the queen's kindred are made gentle-folks:
    How say you sir? Can you deny all this?
BRAKENBURY
    With this, my lord, myself have nought to do.
GLOUCESTER
    Naught to do with mistress Shore! I tell thee, fellow,
    He that doth naught with her, excepting one,
    Were best he do it secretly, alone.
BRAKENBURY
    What one, my lord?
GLOUCESTER
    Her husband, knave: wouldst thou betray me?
BRAKENBURY
    I beseech your grace to pardon me, and withal
    Forbear your conference with the noble duke.
CLARENCE
    We know thy charge, Brakenbury, and will obey.

The Tragedy of Richard the Third— Act I

GLOUCESTER
   We are the queen's abjects, and must obey.
   Brother, farewell: I will unto the king;
   And whatsoever you will employ me in,
   Were it to call King Edward's widow sister,
   I will perform it to enfranchise you.
   Meantime, this deep disgrace in brotherhood
   Touches me deeper than you can imagine.
CLARENCE
   I know it pleaseth neither of us well.
GLOUCESTER
   Well, your imprisonment shall not be long;
   Meantime, have patience.
CLARENCE
   I must perforce. Farewell.

   Exeunt CLARENCE, BRAKENBURY, and Guard

GLOUCESTER
   Go, tread the path that thou shalt ne'er return.
   Simple, plain Clarence! I do love thee so,
   That I will shortly send thy soul to heaven,
   If heaven will take the present at our hands.
   But who comes here? the new-deliver'd Hastings?

   Enter HASTINGS

HASTINGS
   Good time of day unto my gracious lord!
GLOUCESTER
   As much unto my good lord chamberlain!
   Well are you welcome to the open air.
   How hath your lordship brook'd imprisonment?
HASTINGS
   With patience, noble lord, as prisoners must:

The Tragedy of Richard the Third— Act I

But I shall live, my lord, to give them thanks
That were the cause of my imprisonment.
GLOUCESTER
No doubt, no doubt; and so shall Clarence too;
For they that were your enemies are his,
And have prevail'd as much on him as you.
HASTINGS
More pity that the eagle should be mew'd,
While kites and buzzards prey at liberty.
GLOUCESTER
What news abroad?
HASTINGS
No news so bad abroad as this at home;
The King is sickly, weak and melancholy,
And his physicians fear him mightily.
GLOUCESTER
Now, by Saint Paul, this news is bad indeed.
O, he hath kept an evil diet long,
And overmuch consumed his royal person:
'Tis very grievous to be thought upon.
What, is he in his bed?
HASTINGS
He is.
GLOUCESTER
Go you before, and I will follow you.

Exit HASTINGS

He cannot live, I hope; and must not die
Till George be pack'd with post-horse up to heaven.
I'll in, to urge his hatred more to Clarence,
With lies well steel'd with weighty arguments;
And, if I fall not in my deep intent,
Clarence hath not another day to live:
Which done, God take King Edward to his mercy,

The Tragedy of Richard the Third— Act I

And leave the world for me to bustle in!
For then I'll marry Warwick's youngest daughter.
What though I kill'd her husband and her father?
The readiest way to make the wench amends
Is to become her husband and her father:
The which will I; not all so much for love
As for another secret close intent,
By marrying her which I must reach unto.
But yet I run before my horse to market:
Clarence still breathes; Edward still lives and reigns:
When they are gone, then must I count my gains.

Exit

SCENE II.
The same. Another street.

Enter the corpse of KING HENRY the Sixth, Gentlemen with halberds to guard it; LADY ANNE being the mourner

LADY ANNE
Set down, set down your honourable load,
If honour may be shrouded in a hearse,
Whilst I awhile obsequiously lament
The untimely fall of virtuous Lancaster.
Poor key-cold figure of a holy king!
Pale ashes of the house of Lancaster!
Thou bloodless remnant of that royal blood!
Be it lawful that I invocate thy ghost,
To hear the lamentations of Poor Anne,
Wife to thy Edward, to thy slaughter'd son,
Stabb'd by the selfsame hand that made these wounds!
Lo, in these windows that let forth thy life,
I pour the helpless balm of my poor eyes.

The Tragedy of Richard the Third— Act I

Cursed be the hand that made these fatal holes!
Cursed be the heart that had the heart to do it!
Cursed the blood that let this blood from hence!
More direful hap betide that hated wretch,
That makes us wretched by the death of thee,
Than I can wish to adders, spiders, toads,
Or any creeping venom'd thing that lives!
If ever he have child, abortive be it,
Prodigious, and untimely brought to light,
Whose ugly and unnatural aspect
May fright the hopeful mother at the view;
And that be heir to his unhappiness!
If ever he have wife, let her he made
A miserable by the death of him
As I am made by my poor lord and thee!
Come, now towards Chertsey with your holy load,
Taken from Paul's to be interred there;
And still, as you are weary of the weight,
Rest you, whiles I lament King Henry's corse.

Enter GLOUCESTER

GLOUCESTER
Stay, you that bear the corse, and set it down.
LADY ANNE
What black magician conjures up this fiend,
To stop devoted charitable deeds?
GLOUCESTER
Villains, set down the corse; or, by Saint Paul,
I'll make a corse of him that disobeys.
Gentleman
My lord, stand back, and let the coffin pass.
GLOUCESTER
Unmanner'd dog! stand thou, when I command:
Advance thy halbert higher than my breast,

The Tragedy of Richard the Third— Act I

Or, by Saint Paul, I'll strike thee to my foot,
And spurn upon thee, beggar, for thy boldness.
LADY ANNE
What, do you tremble? are you all afraid?
Alas, I blame you not; for you are mortal,
And mortal eyes cannot endure the devil.
Avaunt, thou dreadful minister of hell!
Thou hadst but power over his mortal body,
His soul thou canst not have; therefore be gone.
GLOUCESTER
Sweet saint, for charity, be not so curst.
LADY ANNE
Foul devil, for God's sake, hence, and trouble us not;
For thou hast made the happy earth thy hell,
Fill'd it with cursing cries and deep exclaims.
If thou delight to view thy heinous deeds,
Behold this pattern of thy butcheries.
O, gentlemen, see, see! dead Henry's wounds
Open their congeal'd mouths and bleed afresh!
Blush, Blush, thou lump of foul deformity;
For 'tis thy presence that exhales this blood
From cold and empty veins, where no blood dwells;
Thy deed, inhuman and unnatural,
Provokes this deluge most unnatural.
O God, which this blood madest, revenge his death!
O earth, which this blood drink'st revenge his death!
Either heaven with lightning strike the
murderer dead,
Or earth, gape open wide and eat him quick,
As thou dost swallow up this good king's blood
Which his hell-govern'd arm hath butchered!
GLOUCESTER
Lady, you know no rules of charity,
Which renders good for bad, blessings for curses.

The Tragedy of Richard the Third— Act I

LADY ANNE
   Villain, thou know'st no law of God nor man:
   No beast so fierce but knows some touch of pity.
GLOUCESTER
   But I know none, and therefore am no beast.
LADY ANNE
   O wonderful, when devils tell the truth!
GLOUCESTER
   More wonderful, when angels are so angry.
   Vouchsafe, divine perfection of a woman,
   Of these supposed-evils, to give me leave,
   By circumstance, but to acquit myself.
LADY ANNE
   Vouchsafe, defused infection of a man,
   For these known evils, but to give me leave,
   By circumstance, to curse thy cursed self.
GLOUCESTER
   Fairer than tongue can name thee, let me have
   Some patient leisure to excuse myself.
LADY ANNE
   Fouler than heart can think thee, thou canst make
   No excuse current, but to hang thyself.
GLOUCESTER
   By such despair, I should accuse myself.
LADY ANNE
   And, by despairing, shouldst thou stand excused;
   For doing worthy vengeance on thyself,
   Which didst unworthy slaughter upon others.
GLOUCESTER
   Say that I slew them not?
LADY ANNE
   Why, then they are not dead:
   But dead they are, and devilish slave, by thee.

The Tragedy of Richard the Third— Act I

GLOUCESTER
  I did not kill your husband.
LADY ANNE
  Why, then he is alive.
GLOUCESTER
  Nay, he is dead; and slain by Edward's hand.
LADY ANNE
  In thy foul throat thou liest: Queen Margaret saw
  Thy murderous falchion smoking in his blood;
  The which thou once didst bend against her breast,
  But that thy brothers beat aside the point.
GLOUCESTER
  I was provoked by her slanderous tongue,
  which laid their guilt upon my guiltless shoulders.
LADY ANNE
  Thou wast provoked by thy bloody mind.
  Which never dreamt on aught but butcheries:
  Didst thou not kill this king?
GLOUCESTER
  I grant ye.
LADY ANNE
  Dost grant me, hedgehog? then, God grant me too
  Thou mayst be damned for that wicked deed!
  O, he was gentle, mild, and virtuous!
GLOUCESTER
  The fitter for the King of heaven, that hath him.
LADY ANNE
  He is in heaven, where thou shalt never come.
GLOUCESTER
  Let him thank me, that holp to send him thither;
  For he was fitter for that place than earth.
LADY ANNE
  And thou unfit for any place but hell.

The Tragedy of Richard the Third— Act I

GLOUCESTER
　Yes, one place else, if you will hear me name it.
LADY ANNE
　Some dungeon.
GLOUCESTER
　Your bed-chamber.
LADY ANNE
　Ill rest betide the chamber where thou liest!
GLOUCESTER
　So will it, madam till I lie with you.
LADY ANNE
　I hope so.
GLOUCESTER
　I know so. But, gentle Lady Anne,
　To leave this keen encounter of our wits,
　And fall somewhat into a slower method,
　Is not the causer of the timeless deaths
　Of these Plantagenets, Henry and Edward,
　As blameful as the executioner?
LADY ANNE
　Thou art the cause, and most accursed effect.
GLOUCESTER
　Your beauty was the cause of that effect;
　Your beauty: which did haunt me in my sleep
　To undertake the death of all the world,
　So I might live one hour in your sweet bosom.
LADY ANNE
　If I thought that, I tell thee, homicide,
　These nails should rend that beauty from my cheeks.
GLOUCESTER
　These eyes could never endure sweet beauty's wreck;
　You should not blemish it, if I stood by:
　As all the world is cheered by the sun,
　So I by that; it is my day, my life.

LADY ANNE
  Black night o'ershade thy day, and death thy life!
GLOUCESTER
  Curse not thyself, fair creature thou art both.
LADY ANNE
  I would I were, to be revenged on thee.
GLOUCESTER
  It is a quarrel most unnatural,
  To be revenged on him that loveth you.
LADY ANNE
  It is a quarrel just and reasonable,
  To be revenged on him that slew my husband.
GLOUCESTER
  He that bereft thee, lady, of thy husband,
  Did it to help thee to a better husband.
LADY ANNE
  His better doth not breathe upon the earth.
GLOUCESTER
  He lives that loves thee better than he could.
LADY ANNE
  Name him.
GLOUCESTER
  Plantagenet.
LADY ANNE
  Why, that was he.
GLOUCESTER
  The selfsame name, but one of better nature.
LADY ANNE
  Where is he?
GLOUCESTER
  Here.

She spitteth at him

  Why dost thou spit at me?

The Tragedy of Richard the Third— Act I

LADY ANNE
  Would it were mortal poison, for thy sake!
GLOUCESTER
  Never came poison from so sweet a place.
LADY ANNE
  Never hung poison on a fouler toad.
  Out of my sight! thou dost infect my eyes.
GLOUCESTER
  Thine eyes, sweet lady, have infected mine.
LADY ANNE
  Would they were basilisks, to strike thee dead!
GLOUCESTER
  I would they were, that I might die at once;
  For now they kill me with a living death.
  Those eyes of thine from mine have drawn salt tears,
  Shamed their aspect with store of childish drops:
  These eyes that never shed remorseful tear,
  No, when my father York and Edward wept,
  To hear the piteous moan that Rutland made
  When black-faced Clifford shook his sword at him;
  Nor when thy warlike father, like a child,
  Told the sad story of my father's death,
  And twenty times made pause to sob and weep,
  That all the standers-by had wet their cheeks
  Like trees bedash'd with rain: in that sad time
  My manly eyes did scorn an humble tear;
  And what these sorrows could not thence exhale,
  Thy beauty hath, and made them blind with weeping.
  I never sued to friend nor enemy;
  My tongue could never learn sweet smoothing word;
  But now thy beauty is proposed my fee,
  My proud heart sues, and prompts my tongue to speak.

   She looks scornfully at him

The Tragedy of Richard the Third— Act I

Teach not thy lips such scorn, for they were made
For kissing, lady, not for such contempt.
If thy revengeful heart cannot forgive,
Lo, here I lend thee this sharp-pointed sword;
Which if thou please to hide in this true bosom.
And let the soul forth that adoreth thee,
I lay it naked to the deadly stroke,
And humbly beg the death upon my knee.

He lays his breast open: she offers at it with his sword

Nay, do not pause; for I did kill King Henry,
But 'twas thy beauty that provoked me.
Nay, now dispatch; 'twas I that stabb'd young Edward,
But 'twas thy heavenly face that set me on.

Here she lets fall the sword

Take up the sword again, or take up me.
LADY ANNE
Arise, dissembler: though I wish thy death,
I will not be the executioner.
GLOUCESTER
Then bid me kill myself, and I will do it.
LADY ANNE
I have already.
GLOUCESTER
Tush, that was in thy rage:
Speak it again, and, even with the word,
That hand, which, for thy love, did kill thy love,
Shall, for thy love, kill a far truer love;
To both their deaths thou shalt be accessary.
LADY ANNE
I would I knew thy heart.

The Tragedy of Richard the Third— Act I

GLOUCESTER
  'Tis figured in my tongue.
LADY ANNE
  I fear me both are false.
GLOUCESTER
  Then never man was true.
LADY ANNE
  Well, well, put up your sword.
GLOUCESTER
  Say, then, my peace is made.
LADY ANNE
  That shall you know hereafter.
GLOUCESTER
  But shall I live in hope?
LADY ANNE
  All men, I hope, live so.
GLOUCESTER
  Vouchsafe to wear this ring.
LADY ANNE
  To take is not to give.
GLOUCESTER
  Look, how this ring encompasseth finger.
  Even so thy breast encloseth my poor heart;
  Wear both of them, for both of them are thine.
  And if thy poor devoted suppliant may
  But beg one favour at thy gracious hand,
  Thou dost confirm his happiness for ever.
LADY ANNE
  What is it?
GLOUCESTER
  That it would please thee leave these sad designs
  To him that hath more cause to be a mourner,
  And presently repair to Crosby Place;
  Where, after I have solemnly interr'd

The Tragedy of Richard the Third— Act I

At Chertsey monastery this noble king,
And wet his grave with my repentant tears,
I will with all expedient duty see you:
For divers unknown reasons. I beseech you,
Grant me this boon.

LADY ANNE
With all my heart; and much it joys me too,
To see you are become so penitent.
Tressel and Berkeley, go along with me.

GLOUCESTER
Bid me farewell.

LADY ANNE
'Tis more than you deserve;
But since you teach me how to flatter you,
Imagine I have said farewell already.

Exeunt LADY ANNE, TRESSEL, and BERKELEY

GLOUCESTER
Sirs, take up the corse.

GENTLEMEN
Towards Chertsey, noble lord?

GLOUCESTER
No, to White-Friars; there attend my coining.

Exeunt all but GLOUCESTER

Was ever woman in this humour woo'd?
Was ever woman in this humour won?
I'll have her; but I will not keep her long.
What! I, that kill'd her husband and his father,
To take her in her heart's extremest hate,
With curses in her mouth, tears in her eyes,
The bleeding witness of her hatred by;
Having God, her conscience, and these bars

The Tragedy of Richard the Third— Act I

against me,
And I nothing to back my suit at all,
But the plain devil and dissembling looks,
And yet to win her, all the world to nothing!
Ha!
Hath she forgot already that brave prince,
Edward, her lord, whom I, some three months since,
Stabb'd in my angry mood at Tewksbury?
A sweeter and a lovelier gentleman,
Framed in the prodigality of nature,
Young, valiant, wise, and, no doubt, right royal,
The spacious world cannot again afford
And will she yet debase her eyes on me,
That cropp'd the golden prime of this sweet prince,
And made her widow to a woful bed?
On me, whose all not equals Edward's moiety?
On me, that halt and am unshapen thus?
My dukedom to a beggarly denier,
I do mistake my person all this while:
Upon my life, she finds, although I cannot,
Myself to be a marvellous proper man.
I'll be at charges for a looking-glass,
And entertain some score or two of tailors,
To study fashions to adorn my body:
Since I am crept in favour with myself,
Will maintain it with some little cost.
But first I'll turn yon fellow in his grave;
And then return lamenting to my love.
Shine out, fair sun, till I have bought a glass,
That I may see my shadow as I pass.

Exit

The Tragedy of Richard the Third— Act I

SCENE III.
The palace.

Enter QUEEN ELIZABETH, RIVERS, and GREY

RIVERS
 Have patience, madam: there's no doubt his majesty
 Will soon recover his accustom'd health.
GREY
 In that you brook it in, it makes him worse:
 Therefore, for God's sake, entertain good comfort,
 And cheer his grace with quick and merry words.
QUEEN ELIZABETH
 If he were dead, what would betide of me?
RIVERS
 No other harm but loss of such a lord.
QUEEN ELIZABETH
 The loss of such a lord includes all harm.
GREY
 The heavens have bless'd you with a goodly son,
 To be your comforter when he is gone.
QUEEN ELIZABETH
 Oh, he is young and his minority
 Is put unto the trust of Richard Gloucester,
 A man that loves not me, nor none of you.
RIVERS
 Is it concluded that he shall be protector?
QUEEN ELIZABETH
 It is determined, not concluded yet:
 But so it must be, if the king miscarry.

Enter BUCKINGHAM and DERBY

GREY
 Here come the lords of Buckingham and Derby.

The Tragedy of Richard the Third— Act I

BUCKINGHAM
Good time of day unto your royal grace!
DERBY
God make your majesty joyful as you have been!
QUEEN ELIZABETH
The Countess Richmond, good my Lord of Derby.
To your good prayers will scarcely say amen.
Yet, Derby, notwithstanding she's your wife,
And loves not me, be you, good lord, assured
I hate not you for her proud arrogance.
DERBY
I do beseech you, either not believe
The envious slanders of her false accusers;
Or, if she be accused in true report,
Bear with her weakness, which, I think proceeds
From wayward sickness, and no grounded malice.
RIVERS
Saw you the king to-day, my Lord of Derby?
DERBY
But now the Duke of Buckingham and I
Are come from visiting his majesty.
QUEEN ELIZABETH
What likelihood of his amendment, lords?
BUCKINGHAM
Madam, good hope; his grace speaks cheerfully.
QUEEN ELIZABETH
God grant him health! Did you confer with him?
BUCKINGHAM
Madam, we did: he desires to make atonement
Betwixt the Duke of Gloucester and your brothers,
And betwixt them and my lord chamberlain;
And sent to warn them to his royal presence.
QUEEN ELIZABETH
Would all were well! but that will never be

I fear our happiness is at the highest.

Enter GLOUCESTER, HASTINGS, and DORSET

GLOUCESTER
    They do me wrong, and I will not endure it:
    Who are they that complain unto the king,
    That I, forsooth, am stern, and love them not?
    By holy Paul, they love his grace but lightly
    That fill his ears with such dissentious rumours.
    Because I cannot flatter and speak fair,
    Smile in men's faces, smooth, deceive and cog,
    Duck with French nods and apish courtesy,
    I must be held a rancorous enemy.
    Cannot a plain man live and think no harm,
    But thus his simple truth must be abused
    By silken, sly, insinuating Jacks?
RIVERS
    To whom in all this presence speaks your grace?
GLOUCESTER
    To thee, that hast nor honesty nor grace.
    When have I injured thee? when done thee wrong?
    Or thee? or thee? or any of your faction?
    A plague upon you all! His royal person,--
    Whom God preserve better than you would wish!--
    Cannot be quiet scarce a breathing-while,
    But you must trouble him with lewd complaints.
QUEEN ELIZABETH
    Brother of Gloucester, you mistake the matter.
    The king, of his own royal disposition,
    And not provoked by any suitor else;
    Aiming, belike, at your interior hatred,
    Which in your outward actions shows itself
    Against my kindred, brothers, and myself,
    Makes him to send; that thereby he may gather

The Tragedy of Richard the Third— Act I

   The ground of your ill-will, and so remove it.
GLOUCESTER
   I cannot tell: the world is grown so bad,
   That wrens make prey where eagles dare not perch:
   Since every Jack became a gentleman
   There's many a gentle person made a Jack.
QUEEN ELIZABETH
   Come, come, we know your meaning, brother Gloucester;
   You envy my advancement and my friends':
   God grant we never may have need of you!
GLOUCESTER
   Meantime, God grants that we have need of you:
   Your brother is imprison'd by your means,
   Myself disgraced, and the nobility
   Held in contempt; whilst many fair promotions
   Are daily given to ennoble those
   That scarce, some two days since, were worth a noble.
QUEEN ELIZABETH
   By Him that raised me to this careful height
   From that contented hap which I enjoy'd,
   I never did incense his majesty
   Against the Duke of Clarence, but have been
   An earnest advocate to plead for him.
   My lord, you do me shameful injury,
   Falsely to draw me in these vile suspects.
GLOUCESTER
   You may deny that you were not the cause
   Of my Lord Hastings' late imprisonment.
RIVERS
   She may, my lord, for--
GLOUCESTER
   She may, Lord Rivers! why, who knows not so?
   She may do more, sir, than denying that:

The Tragedy of Richard the Third— Act I

    She may help you to many fair preferments,
    And then deny her aiding hand therein,
    And lay those honours on your high deserts.
    What may she not? She may, yea, marry, may she--
RIVERS
    What, marry, may she?
GLOUCESTER
    What, marry, may she! marry with a king,
    A bachelor, a handsome stripling too:
    I wis your grandam had a worser match.
QUEEN ELIZABETH
    My Lord of Gloucester, I have too long borne
    Your blunt upbraidings and your bitter scoffs:
    By heaven, I will acquaint his majesty
    With those gross taunts I often have endured.
    I had rather be a country servant-maid
    Than a great queen, with this condition,
    To be thus taunted, scorn'd, and baited at:

              Enter QUEEN MARGARET, behind

    Small joy have I in being England's queen.

QUEEN MARGARET
    And lessen'd be that small, God, I beseech thee!
    Thy honour, state and seat is due to me.
GLOUCESTER
    What! threat you me with telling of the king?
    Tell him, and spare not: look, what I have said
    I will avouch in presence of the king:
    I dare adventure to be sent to the Tower.
    'Tis time to speak; my pains are quite forgot.
QUEEN MARGARET
    Out, devil! I remember them too well:
    Thou slewest my husband Henry in the Tower,

And Edward, my poor son, at Tewksbury.
GLOUCESTER
   Ere you were queen, yea, or your husband king,
   I was a pack-horse in his great affairs;
   A weeder-out of his proud adversaries,
   A liberal rewarder of his friends:
   To royalize his blood I spilt mine own.
QUEEN MARGARET
   Yea, and much better blood than his or thine.
GLOUCESTER
   In all which time you and your husband Grey
   Were factious for the house of Lancaster;
   And, Rivers, so were you. Was not your husband
   In Margaret's battle at Saint Alban's slain?
   Let me put in your minds, if you forget,
   What you have been ere now, and what you are;
   Withal, what I have been, and what I am.
QUEEN MARGARET
   A murderous villain, and so still thou art.
GLOUCESTER
   Poor Clarence did forsake his father, Warwick;
   Yea, and forswore himself,--which Jesu pardon!--
QUEEN MARGARET
   Which God revenge!
GLOUCESTER
   To fight on Edward's party for the crown;
   And for his meed, poor lord, he is mew'd up.
   I would to God my heart were flint, like Edward's;
   Or Edward's soft and pitiful, like mine
   I am too childish-foolish for this world.
QUEEN MARGARET
   Hie thee to hell for shame, and leave the world,
   Thou cacodemon! there thy kingdom is.

RIVERS
>My Lord of Gloucester, in those busy days
>Which here you urge to prove us enemies,
>We follow'd then our lord, our lawful king:
>So should we you, if you should be our king.

GLOUCESTER
>If I should be! I had rather be a pedlar:
>Far be it from my heart, the thought of it!

QUEEN ELIZABETH
>As little joy, my lord, as you suppose
>You should enjoy, were you this country's king,
>As little joy may you suppose in me.
>That I enjoy, being the queen thereof.

QUEEN MARGARET
>A little joy enjoys the queen thereof;
>For I am she, and altogether joyless.
>I can no longer hold me patient.

Advancing

>Hear me, you wrangling pirates, that fall out
>In sharing that which you have pill'd from me!
>Which of you trembles not that looks on me?
>If not, that, I being queen, you bow like subjects,
>Yet that, by you deposed, you quake like rebels?
>O gentle villain, do not turn away!

GLOUCESTER
>Foul wrinkled witch, what makest thou in my sight?

QUEEN MARGARET
>But repetition of what thou hast marr'd;
>That will I make before I let thee go.

GLOUCESTER
>Wert thou not banished on pain of death?

QUEEN MARGARET
>I was; but I do find more pain in banishment

The Tragedy of Richard the Third— Act I

    Than death can yield me here by my abode.
    A husband and a son thou owest to me;
    And thou a kingdom; all of you allegiance:
    The sorrow that I have, by right is yours,
    And all the pleasures you usurp are mine.
GLOUCESTER
    The curse my noble father laid on thee,
    When thou didst crown his warlike brows with paper
    And with thy scorns drew'st rivers from his eyes,
    And then, to dry them, gavest the duke a clout
    Steep'd in the faultless blood of pretty Rutland--
    His curses, then from bitterness of soul
    Denounced against thee, are all fall'n upon thee;
    And God, not we, hath plagued thy bloody deed.
QUEEN ELIZABETH
    So just is God, to right the innocent.
HASTINGS
    O, 'twas the foulest deed to slay that babe,
    And the most merciless that e'er was heard of!
RIVERS
    Tyrants themselves wept when it was reported.
DORSET
    No man but prophesied revenge for it.
BUCKINGHAM
    Northumberland, then present, wept to see it.
QUEEN MARGARET
    What were you snarling all before I came,
    Ready to catch each other by the throat,
    And turn you all your hatred now on me?
    Did York's dread curse prevail so much with heaven?
    That Henry's death, my lovely Edward's death,
    Their kingdom's loss, my woful banishment,
    Could all but answer for that peevish brat?
    Can curses pierce the clouds and enter heaven?

The Tragedy of Richard the Third— Act I

Why, then, give way, dull clouds, to my quick curses!
If not by war, by surfeit die your king,
As ours by murder, to make him a king!
Edward thy son, which now is Prince of Wales,
For Edward my son, which was Prince of Wales,
Die in his youth by like untimely violence!
Thyself a queen, for me that was a queen,
Outlive thy glory, like my wretched self!
Long mayst thou live to wail thy children's loss;
And see another, as I see thee now,
Deck'd in thy rights, as thou art stall'd in mine!
Long die thy happy days before thy death;
And, after many lengthen'd hours of grief,
Die neither mother, wife, nor England's queen!
Rivers and Dorset, you were standers by,
And so wast thou, Lord Hastings, when my son
Was stabb'd with bloody daggers: God, I pray him,
That none of you may live your natural age,
But by some unlook'd accident cut off!

GLOUCESTER

Have done thy charm, thou hateful wither'd hag!

QUEEN MARGARET

And leave out thee? stay, dog, for thou shalt hear me.
If heaven have any grievous plague in store
Exceeding those that I can wish upon thee,
O, let them keep it till thy sins be ripe,
And then hurl down their indignation
On thee, the troubler of the poor world's peace!
The worm of conscience still begnaw thy soul!
Thy friends suspect for traitors while thou livest,
And take deep traitors for thy dearest friends!
No sleep close up that deadly eye of thine,
Unless it be whilst some tormenting dream
Affrights thee with a hell of ugly devils!

The Tragedy of Richard the Third— Act I

   Thou elvish-mark'd, abortive, rooting hog!
   Thou that wast seal'd in thy nativity
   The slave of nature and the son of hell!
   Thou slander of thy mother's heavy womb!
   Thou loathed issue of thy father's loins!
   Thou rag of honour! thou detested--
GLOUCESTER
   Margaret.
QUEEN MARGARET
   Richard!
GLOUCESTER
   Ha!
QUEEN MARGARET
   I call thee not.
GLOUCESTER
   I cry thee mercy then, for I had thought
   That thou hadst call'd me all these bitter names.
QUEEN MARGARET
   Why, so I did; but look'd for no reply.
   O, let me make the period to my curse!
GLOUCESTER
   'Tis done by me, and ends in 'Margaret.'
QUEEN ELIZABETH
   Thus have you breathed your curse against yourself.
QUEEN MARGARET
   Poor painted queen, vain flourish of my fortune!
   Why strew'st thou sugar on that bottled spider,
   Whose deadly web ensnareth thee about?
   Fool, fool! thou whet'st a knife to kill thyself.
   The time will come when thou shalt wish for me
   To help thee curse that poisonous bunchback'd toad.
HASTINGS
   False-boding woman, end thy frantic curse,
   Lest to thy harm thou move our patience.

The Tragedy of Richard the Third— Act I

QUEEN MARGARET
  Foul shame upon you! you have all moved mine.
RIVERS
  Were you well served, you would be taught your duty.
QUEEN MARGARET
  To serve me well, you all should do me duty,
  Teach me to be your queen, and you my subjects:
  O, serve me well, and teach yourselves that duty!
DORSET
  Dispute not with her; she is lunatic.
QUEEN MARGARET
  Peace, master marquess, you are malapert:
  Your fire-new stamp of honour is scarce current.
  O, that your young nobility could judge
  What 'twere to lose it, and be miserable!
  They that stand high have many blasts to shake them;
  And if they fall, they dash themselves to pieces.
GLOUCESTER
  Good counsel, marry: learn it, learn it, marquess.
DORSET
  It toucheth you, my lord, as much as me.
GLOUCESTER
  Yea, and much more: but I was born so high,
  Our aery buildeth in the cedar's top,
  And dallies with the wind and scorns the sun.
QUEEN MARGARET
  And turns the sun to shade; alas! alas!
  Witness my son, now in the shade of death;
  Whose bright out-shining beams thy cloudy wrath
  Hath in eternal darkness folded up.
  Your aery buildeth in our aery's nest.
  O God, that seest it, do not suffer it!
  As it was won with blood, lost be it so!

The Tragedy of Richard the Third— Act I

BUCKINGHAM
  Have done! for shame, if not for charity.
QUEEN MARGARET
  Urge neither charity nor shame to me:
  Uncharitably with me have you dealt,
  And shamefully by you my hopes are butcher'd.
  My charity is outrage, life my shame
  And in that shame still live my sorrow's rage.
BUCKINGHAM
  Have done, have done.
QUEEN MARGARET
  O princely Buckingham I'll kiss thy hand,
  In sign of league and amity with thee:
  Now fair befal thee and thy noble house!
  Thy garments are not spotted with our blood,
  Nor thou within the compass of my curse.
BUCKINGHAM
  Nor no one here; for curses never pass
  The lips of those that breathe them in the air.
QUEEN MARGARET
  I'll not believe but they ascend the sky,
  And there awake God's gentle-sleeping peace.
  O Buckingham, take heed of yonder dog!
  Look, when he fawns, he bites; and when he bites,
  His venom tooth will rankle to the death:
  Have not to do with him, beware of him;
  Sin, death, and hell have set their marks on him,
  And all their ministers attend on him.
GLOUCESTER
  What doth she say, my Lord of Buckingham?
BUCKINGHAM
  Nothing that I respect, my gracious lord.
QUEEN MARGARET
  What, dost thou scorn me for my gentle counsel?

The Tragedy of Richard the Third— Act I

And soothe the devil that I warn thee from?
O, but remember this another day,
When he shall split thy very heart with sorrow,
And say poor Margaret was a prophetess!
Live each of you the subjects to his hate,
And he to yours, and all of you to God's!

Exit

HASTINGS
   My hair doth stand on end to hear her curses.
RIVERS
   And so doth mine: I muse why she's at liberty.
GLOUCESTER
   I cannot blame her: by God's holy mother,
   She hath had too much wrong; and I repent
   My part thereof that I have done to her.
QUEEN ELIZABETH
   I never did her any, to my knowledge.
GLOUCESTER
   But you have all the vantage of her wrong.
   I was too hot to do somebody good,
   That is too cold in thinking of it now.
   Marry, as for Clarence, he is well repaid,
   He is frank'd up to fatting for his pains
   God pardon them that are the cause of it!
RIVERS
   A virtuous and a Christian-like conclusion,
   To pray for them that have done scathe to us.
GLOUCESTER
   So do I ever:

Aside

   being well-advised.
   For had I cursed now, I had cursed myself.

The Tragedy of Richard the Third— Act I

Enter CATESBY

CATESBY
  Madam, his majesty doth call for you,
  And for your grace; and you, my noble lords.
QUEEN ELIZABETH
  Catesby, we come. Lords, will you go with us?
RIVERS
  Madam, we will attend your grace.

Exeunt all but GLOUCESTER

GLOUCESTER
  I do the wrong, and first begin to brawl.
  The secret mischiefs that I set abroach
  I lay unto the grievous charge of others.
  Clarence, whom I, indeed, have laid in darkness,
  I do beweep to many simple gulls
  Namely, to Hastings, Derby, Buckingham;
  And say it is the queen and her allies
  That stir the king against the duke my brother.
  Now, they believe it; and withal whet me
  To be revenged on Rivers, Vaughan, Grey:
  But then I sigh; and, with a piece of scripture,
  Tell them that God bids us do good for evil:
  And thus I clothe my naked villany
  With old odd ends stolen out of holy writ;
  And seem a saint, when most I play the devil.

Enter two Murderers

  But, soft! here come my executioners.
  How now, my hardy, stout resolved mates!
  Are you now going to dispatch this deed?

The Tragedy of Richard the Third— Act I

First Murderer
  We are, my lord; and come to have the warrant
  That we may be admitted where he is.
GLOUCESTER
  Well thought upon; I have it here about me.

Gives the warrant

  When you have done, repair to Crosby Place.
  But, sirs, be sudden in the execution,
  Withal obdurate, do not hear him plead;
  For Clarence is well-spoken, and perhaps
  May move your hearts to pity if you mark him.
First Murderer
  Tush!
  Fear not, my lord, we will not stand to prate;
  Talkers are no good doers: be assured
  We come to use our hands and not our tongues.
GLOUCESTER
  Your eyes drop millstones, when fools' eyes drop tears:
  I like you, lads; about your business straight;
  Go, go, dispatch.
First Murderer
  We will, my noble lord.

Exeunt

SCENE IV.
London. The Tower.

Enter CLARENCE and BRAKENBURY

BRAKENBURY
  Why looks your grace so heavily today?

The Tragedy of Richard the Third— Act I

CLARENCE
   O, I have pass'd a miserable night,
   So full of ugly sights, of ghastly dreams,
   That, as I am a Christian faithful man,
   I would not spend another such a night,
   Though 'twere to buy a world of happy days,
   So full of dismal terror was the time!

BRAKENBURY
   What was your dream? I long to hear you tell it.

CLARENCE
   Methoughts that I had broken from the Tower,
   And was embark'd to cross to Burgundy;
   And, in my company, my brother Gloucester;
   Who from my cabin tempted me to walk
   Upon the hatches: thence we looked toward England,
   And cited up a thousand fearful times,
   During the wars of York and Lancaster
   That had befall'n us. As we paced along
   Upon the giddy footing of the hatches,
   Methought that Gloucester stumbled; and, in falling,
   Struck me, that thought to stay him, overboard,
   Into the tumbling billows of the main.
   Lord, Lord! methought, what pain it was to drown!
   What dreadful noise of waters in mine ears!
   What ugly sights of death within mine eyes!
   Methought I saw a thousand fearful wrecks;
   Ten thousand men that fishes gnaw'd upon;
   Wedges of gold, great anchors, heaps of pearl,
   Inestimable stones, unvalued jewels,
   All scatter'd in the bottom of the sea:
   Some lay in dead men's skulls; and, in those holes
   Where eyes did once inhabit, there were crept,
   As 'twere in scorn of eyes, reflecting gems,
   Which woo'd the slimy bottom of the deep,

The Tragedy of Richard the Third— Act I

    And mock'd the dead bones that lay scatter'd by.
BRAKENBURY
    Had you such leisure in the time of death
    To gaze upon the secrets of the deep?
CLARENCE
    Methought I had; and often did I strive
    To yield the ghost: but still the envious flood
    Kept in my soul, and would not let it forth
    To seek the empty, vast and wandering air;
    But smother'd it within my panting bulk,
    Which almost burst to belch it in the sea.
BRAKENBURY
    Awaked you not with this sore agony?
CLARENCE
    O, no, my dream was lengthen'd after life;
    O, then began the tempest to my soul,
    Who pass'd, methought, the melancholy flood,
    With that grim ferryman which poets write of,
    Unto the kingdom of perpetual night.
    The first that there did greet my stranger soul,
    Was my great father-in-law, renowned Warwick;
    Who cried aloud, 'What scourge for perjury
    Can this dark monarchy afford false Clarence?'
    And so he vanish'd: then came wandering by
    A shadow like an angel, with bright hair
    Dabbled in blood; and he squeak'd out aloud,
    'Clarence is come; false, fleeting, perjured Clarence,
    That stabb'd me in the field by Tewksbury;
    Seize on him, Furies, take him to your torments!'
    With that, methoughts, a legion of foul fiends
    Environ'd me about, and howled in mine ears
    Such hideous cries, that with the very noise
    I trembling waked, and for a season after
    Could not believe but that I was in hell,

The Tragedy of Richard the Third— Act I

    Such terrible impression made the dream.
BRAKENBURY
    No marvel, my lord, though it affrighted you;
    I promise, I am afraid to hear you tell it.
CLARENCE
    O Brakenbury, I have done those things,
    Which now bear evidence against my soul,
    For Edward's sake; and see how he requites me!
    O God! if my deep prayers cannot appease thee,
    But thou wilt be avenged on my misdeeds,
    Yet execute thy wrath in me alone,
    O, spare my guiltless wife and my poor children!
    I pray thee, gentle keeper, stay by me;
    My soul is heavy, and I fain would sleep.
BRAKENBURY
    I will, my lord: God give your grace good rest!

CLARENCE sleeps

    Sorrow breaks seasons and reposing hours,
    Makes the night morning, and the noon-tide night.
    Princes have but their tides for their glories,
    An outward honour for an inward toil;
    And, for unfelt imagination,
    They often feel a world of restless cares:
    So that, betwixt their tides and low names,
    There's nothing differs but the outward fame.

Enter the two Murderers

First Murderer
    Ho! who's here?
BRAKENBURY
    In God's name what are you, and how came you hither?

The Tragedy of Richard the Third— Act I

First Murderer
  I would speak with Clarence, and I came hither on my legs.
BRAKENBURY
  Yea, are you so brief?
Second Murderer
  O sir, it is better to be brief than tedious. Show
  him our commission; talk no more.

BRAKENBURY reads it

BRAKENBURY
  I am, in this, commanded to deliver
  The noble Duke of Clarence to your hands:
  I will not reason what is meant hereby,
  Because I will be guiltless of the meaning.
  Here are the keys, there sits the duke asleep:
  I'll to the king; and signify to him
  That thus I have resign'd my charge to you.
First Murderer
  Do so, it is a point of wisdom: fare you well.

Exit BRAKENBURY

Second Murderer
  What, shall we stab him as he sleeps?
First Murderer
  No; then he will say 'twas done cowardly, when he wakes.
Second Murderer
  When he wakes! why, fool, he shall never wake till
  the judgment-day.
First Murderer
  Why, then he will say we stabbed him sleeping.
Second Murderer
  The urging of that word 'judgment' hath bred a kind
  of remorse in me.

The Tragedy of Richard the Third— Act I

First Murderer
  What, art thou afraid?
Second Murderer
  Not to kill him, having a warrant for it; but to be
  damned for killing him, from which no warrant can defend
us.
First Murderer
  I thought thou hadst been resolute.
Second Murderer
  So I am, to let him live.
First Murderer
  Back to the Duke of Gloucester, tell him so.
Second Murderer
  I pray thee, stay a while: I hope my holy humour
  will change; 'twas wont to hold me but while one
  would tell twenty.
First Murderer
  How dost thou feel thyself now?
Second Murderer
  'Faith, some certain dregs of conscience are yet
  within me.
First Murderer
  Remember our reward, when the deed is done.
Second Murderer
  'Zounds, he dies: I had forgot the reward.
First Murderer
  Where is thy conscience now?
Second Murderer
  In the Duke of Gloucester's purse.
First Murderer
  So when he opens his purse to give us our reward,
  thy conscience flies out.
Second Murderer
  Let it go; there's few or none will entertain it.

The Tragedy of Richard the Third— Act I

First Murderer
　How if it come to thee again?
Second Murderer
　I'll not meddle with it: it is a dangerous thing: it
　makes a man a coward: a man cannot steal, but it
　accuseth him; he cannot swear, but it cheques him;
　he cannot lie with his neighbour's wife, but it
　detects him: 'tis a blushing shamefast spirit that
　mutinies in a man's bosom; it fills one full of
　obstacles: it made me once restore a purse of gold
　that I found; it beggars any man that keeps it: it
　is turned out of all towns and cities for a
　dangerous thing; and every man that means to live
　well endeavours to trust to himself and to live
　without it.
First Murderer
　'Zounds, it is even now at my elbow, persuading me
　not to kill the duke.
Second Murderer
　Take the devil in thy mind, and relieve him not: he
　would insinuate with thee but to make thee sigh.
First Murderer
　Tut, I am strong-framed, he cannot prevail with me,
　I warrant thee.
Second Murderer
　Spoke like a tail fellow that respects his
　reputation. Come, shall we to this gear?
First Murderer
　Take him over the costard with the hilts of thy
　sword, and then we will chop him in the malmsey-butt
　in the next room.
Second Murderer
　O excellent devise! make a sop of him.

The Tragedy of Richard the Third— Act I

First Murderer
   Hark! he stirs: shall I strike?
Second Murderer
   No, first let's reason with him.
CLARENCE
   Where art thou, keeper? give me a cup of wine.
Second murderer
   You shall have wine enough, my lord, anon.
CLARENCE
   In God's name, what art thou?
Second Murderer
   A man, as you are.
CLARENCE
   But not, as I am, royal.
Second Murderer
   Nor you, as we are, loyal.
CLARENCE
   Thy voice is thunder, but thy looks are humble.
Second Murderer
   My voice is now the king's, my looks mine own.
CLARENCE
   How darkly and how deadly dost thou speak!
   Your eyes do menace me: why look you pale?
   Who sent you hither? Wherefore do you come?
Both
   To, to, to--
CLARENCE
   To murder me?
Both
   Ay, ay.
CLARENCE
   You scarcely have the hearts to tell me so,
   And therefore cannot have the hearts to do it.
   Wherein, my friends, have I offended you?

The Tragedy of Richard the Third— Act I

First Murderer
   Offended us you have not, but the king.
CLARENCE
   I shall be reconciled to him again.
Second Murderer
   Never, my lord; therefore prepare to die.
CLARENCE
   Are you call'd forth from out a world of men
   To slay the innocent? What is my offence?
   Where are the evidence that do accuse me?
   What lawful quest have given their verdict up
   Unto the frowning judge? or who pronounced
   The bitter sentence of poor Clarence' death?
   Before I be convict by course of law,
   To threaten me with death is most unlawful.
   I charge you, as you hope to have redemption
   By Christ's dear blood shed for our grievous sins,
   That you depart and lay no hands on me
   The deed you undertake is damnable.
First Murderer
   What we will do, we do upon command.
Second Murderer
   And he that hath commanded is the king.
CLARENCE
   Erroneous vassal! the great King of kings
   Hath in the tables of his law commanded
   That thou shalt do no murder: and wilt thou, then,
   Spurn at his edict and fulfil a man's?
   Take heed; for he holds vengeance in his hands,
   To hurl upon their heads that break his law.
Second Murderer
   And that same vengeance doth he hurl on thee,
   For false forswearing and for murder too:
   Thou didst receive the holy sacrament,

The Tragedy of Richard the Third— Act I

    To fight in quarrel of the house of Lancaster.
First Murderer
    And, like a traitor to the name of God,
    Didst break that vow; and with thy treacherous blade
    Unrip'dst the bowels of thy sovereign's son.
Second Murderer
    Whom thou wert sworn to cherish and defend.
First Murderer
    How canst thou urge God's dreadful law to us,
    When thou hast broke it in so dear degree?
CLARENCE
    Alas! for whose sake did I that ill deed?
    For Edward, for my brother, for his sake: Why, sirs,
    He sends ye not to murder me for this
    For in this sin he is as deep as I.
    If God will be revenged for this deed.
    O, know you yet, he doth it publicly,
    Take not the quarrel from his powerful arm;
    He needs no indirect nor lawless course
    To cut off those that have offended him.
First Murderer
    Who made thee, then, a bloody minister,
    When gallant-springing brave Plantagenet,
    That princely novice, was struck dead by thee?
CLARENCE
    My brother's love, the devil, and my rage.
First Murderer
    Thy brother's love, our duty, and thy fault,
    Provoke us hither now to slaughter thee.
CLARENCE
    Oh, if you love my brother, hate not me;
    I am his brother, and I love him well.
    If you be hired for meed, go back again,
    And I will send you to my brother Gloucester,

The Tragedy of Richard the Third— Act I

    Who shall reward you better for my life
    Than Edward will for tidings of my death.
Second Murderer
    You are deceived, your brother Gloucester hates you.
CLARENCE
    O, no, he loves me, and he holds me dear:
    Go you to him from me.
Both
    Ay, so we will.
CLARENCE
    Tell him, when that our princely father York
    Bless'd his three sons with his victorious arm,
    And charged us from his soul to love each other,
    He little thought of this divided friendship:
    Bid Gloucester think of this, and he will weep.
First Murderer
    Ay, millstones; as be lesson'd us to weep.
CLARENCE
    O, do not slander him, for he is kind.
First Murderer
    Right,
    As snow in harvest. Thou deceivest thyself:
    'Tis he that sent us hither now to slaughter thee.
CLARENCE
    It cannot be; for when I parted with him,
    He hugg'd me in his arms, and swore, with sobs,
    That he would labour my delivery.
Second Murderer
    Why, so he doth, now he delivers thee
    From this world's thraldom to the joys of heaven.
First Murderer
    Make peace with God, for you must die, my lord.
CLARENCE
    Hast thou that holy feeling in thy soul,

The Tragedy of Richard the Third— Act I

    To counsel me to make my peace with God,
    And art thou yet to thy own soul so blind,
    That thou wilt war with God by murdering me?
    Ah, sirs, consider, he that set you on
    To do this deed will hate you for the deed.
Second Murderer
    What shall we do?
CLARENCE
    Relent, and save your souls.
First Murderer
    Relent! 'tis cowardly and womanish.
CLARENCE
    Not to relent is beastly, savage, devilish.
    Which of you, if you were a prince's son,
    Being pent from liberty, as I am now,
    if two such murderers as yourselves came to you,
    Would not entreat for life?
    My friend, I spy some pity in thy looks:
    O, if thine eye be not a flatterer,
    Come thou on my side, and entreat for me,
    As you would beg, were you in my distress
    A begging prince what beggar pities not?
Second Murderer
    Look behind you, my lord.
First Murderer
    Take that, and that: if all this will not do,

Stabs him

    I'll drown you in the malmsey-butt within.

Exit, with the body

Second Murderer
    A bloody deed, and desperately dispatch'd!

The Tragedy of Richard the Third— Act I

    How fain, like Pilate, would I wash my hands
    Of this most grievous guilty murder done!

Re-enter First Murderer

First Murderer
    How now! what mean'st thou, that thou help'st me not?
    By heavens, the duke shall know how slack thou art!
Second Murderer
    I would he knew that I had saved his brother!
    Take thou the fee, and tell him what I say;
    For I repent me that the duke is slain.

Exit

First Murderer
    So do not I: go, coward as thou art.
    Now must I hide his body in some hole,
    Until the duke take order for his burial:
    And when I have my meed, I must away;
    For this will out, and here I must not stay.

ACT II

SCENE I.
London. The palace.

Flourish. Enter KING EDWARD IV sick, QUEEN ELIZABETH, DORSET, RIVERS, HASTINGS, BUCKINGHAM, GREY, and others

KING EDWARD IV
    Why, so: now have I done a good day's work:
    You peers, continue this united league:
    I every day expect an embassage
    From my Redeemer to redeem me hence;
    And now in peace my soul shall part to heaven,
    Since I have set my friends at peace on earth.
    Rivers and Hastings, take each other's hand;
    Dissemble not your hatred, swear your love.
RIVERS
    By heaven, my heart is purged from grudging hate:
    And with my hand I seal my true heart's love.
HASTINGS
    So thrive I, as I truly swear the like!
KING EDWARD IV
    Take heed you dally not before your king;
    Lest he that is the supreme King of kings
    Confound your hidden falsehood, and award
    Either of you to be the other's end.
HASTINGS
    So prosper I, as I swear perfect love!
RIVERS
    And I, as I love Hastings with my heart!
KING EDWARD IV
    Madam, yourself are not exempt in this,

Nor your son Dorset, Buckingham, nor you;
You have been factious one against the other,
Wife, love Lord Hastings, let him kiss your hand;
And what you do, do it unfeignedly.

QUEEN ELIZABETH
Here, Hastings; I will never more remember
Our former hatred, so thrive I and mine!

KING EDWARD IV
Dorset, embrace him; Hastings, love lord marquess.

DORSET
This interchange of love, I here protest,
Upon my part shall be unviolable.

HASTINGS
And so swear I, my lord

They embrace

KING EDWARD IV
Now, princely Buckingham, seal thou this league
With thy embracements to my wife's allies,
And make me happy in your unity.

BUCKINGHAM
Whenever Buckingham doth turn his hate
On you or yours,

To the Queen

but with all duteous love
Doth cherish you and yours, God punish me
With hate in those where I expect most love!
When I have most need to employ a friend,
And most assured that he is a friend
Deep, hollow, treacherous, and full of guile,
Be he unto me! this do I beg of God,
When I am cold in zeal to yours.

The Tragedy of Richard the Third — Act II

KING EDWARD IV
  A pleasing cordial, princely Buckingham,
  is this thy vow unto my sickly heart.
  There wanteth now our brother Gloucester here,
  To make the perfect period of this peace.
BUCKINGHAM
  And, in good time, here comes the noble duke.

Enter GLOUCESTER

GLOUCESTER
  Good morrow to my sovereign king and queen:
  And, princely peers, a happy time of day!
KING EDWARD IV
  Happy, indeed, as we have spent the day.
  Brother, we done deeds of charity;
  Made peace enmity, fair love of hate,
  Between these swelling wrong-incensed peers.
GLOUCESTER
  A blessed labour, my most sovereign liege:
  Amongst this princely heap, if any here,
  By false intelligence, or wrong surmise,
  Hold me a foe;
  If I unwittingly, or in my rage,
  Have aught committed that is hardly borne
  By any in this presence, I desire
  To reconcile me to his friendly peace:
  'Tis death to me to be at enmity;
  I hate it, and desire all good men's love.
  First, madam, I entreat true peace of you,
  Which I will purchase with my duteous service;
  Of you, my noble cousin Buckingham,
  If ever any grudge were lodged between us;
  Of you, Lord Rivers, and, Lord Grey, of you;
  That without desert have frown'd on me;

The Tragedy of Richard the Third — Act II

    Dukes, earls, lords, gentlemen; indeed, of all.
    I do not know that Englishman alive
    With whom my soul is any jot at odds
    More than the infant that is born to-night
    I thank my God for my humility.

QUEEN ELIZABETH
    A holy day shall this be kept hereafter:
    I would to God all strifes were well compounded.
    My sovereign liege, I do beseech your majesty
    To take our brother Clarence to your grace.

GLOUCESTER
    Why, madam, have I offer'd love for this
    To be so bouted in this royal presence?
    Who knows not that the noble duke is dead?

They all start

You do him injury to scorn his corse.

RIVERS
    Who knows not he is dead! who knows he is?

QUEEN ELIZABETH
    All seeing heaven, what a world is this!

BUCKINGHAM
    Look I so pale, Lord Dorset, as the rest?

DORSET
    Ay, my good lord; and no one in this presence
    But his red colour hath forsook his cheeks.

KING EDWARD IV
    Is Clarence dead? the order was reversed.

GLOUCESTER
    But he, poor soul, by your first order died,
    And that a winged Mercury did bear:
    Some tardy cripple bore the countermand,
    That came too lag to see him buried.

The Tragedy of Richard the Third — Act II

God grant that some, less noble and less loyal,
Nearer in bloody thoughts, but not in blood,
Deserve not worse than wretched Clarence did,
And yet go current from suspicion!

Enter DERBY

DERBY
A boon, my sovereign, for my service done!
KING EDWARD IV
I pray thee, peace: my soul is full of sorrow.
DERBY
I will not rise, unless your highness grant.
KING EDWARD IV
Then speak at once what is it thou demand'st.
DERBY
The forfeit, sovereign, of my servant's life;
Who slew to-day a righteous gentleman
Lately attendant on the Duke of Norfolk.
KING EDWARD IV
Have a tongue to doom my brother's death,
And shall the same give pardon to a slave?
My brother slew no man; his fault was thought,
And yet his punishment was cruel death.
Who sued to me for him? who, in my rage,
Kneel'd at my feet, and bade me be advised
Who spake of brotherhood? who spake of love?
Who told me how the poor soul did forsake
The mighty Warwick, and did fight for me?
Who told me, in the field by Tewksbury
When Oxford had me down, he rescued me,
And said, 'Dear brother, live, and be a king'?
Who told me, when we both lay in the field
Frozen almost to death, how he did lap me
Even in his own garments, and gave himself,

The Tragedy of Richard the Third — Act II

All thin and naked, to the numb cold night?
All this from my remembrance brutish wrath
Sinfully pluck'd, and not a man of you
Had so much grace to put it in my mind.
But when your carters or your waiting-vassals
Have done a drunken slaughter, and defaced
The precious image of our dear Redeemer,
You straight are on your knees for pardon, pardon;
And I unjustly too, must grant it you
But for my brother not a man would speak,
Nor I, ungracious, speak unto myself
For him, poor soul. The proudest of you all
Have been beholding to him in his life;
Yet none of you would once plead for his life.
O God, I fear thy justice will take hold
On me, and you, and mine, and yours for this!
Come, Hastings, help me to my closet.
Oh, poor Clarence!

Exeunt some with KING EDWARD IV and QUEEN MARGARET

GLOUCESTER
This is the fruit of rashness! Mark'd you not
How that the guilty kindred of the queen
Look'd pale when they did hear of Clarence' death?
O, they did urge it still unto the king!
God will revenge it. But come, let us in,
To comfort Edward with our company.
BUCKINGHAM
We wait upon your grace.

Exeunt

The Tragedy of Richard the Third — Act II

SCENE II.
The palace.

Enter the DUCHESS OF YORK, with the two children of CLARENCE

Boy
  Tell me, good grandam, is our father dead?
DUCHESS OF YORK
  No, boy.
Boy
  Why do you wring your hands, and beat your breast,
  And cry 'O Clarence, my unhappy son!'
Girl
  Why do you look on us, and shake your head,
  And call us wretches, orphans, castaways
  If that our noble father be alive?
DUCHESS OF YORK
  My pretty cousins, you mistake me much;
  I do lament the sickness of the king.
  As loath to lose him, not your father's death;
  It were lost sorrow to wail one that's lost.
Boy
  Then, grandam, you conclude that he is dead.
  The king my uncle is to blame for this:
  God will revenge it; whom I will importune
  With daily prayers all to that effect.
Girl
  And so will I.
DUCHESS OF YORK
  Peace, children, peace! the king doth love you well:
  Incapable and shallow innocents,
  You cannot guess who caused your father's death.

The Tragedy of Richard the Third — Act II

Boy
>Grandam, we can; for my good uncle Gloucester
>Told me, the king, provoked by the queen,
>Devised impeachments to imprison him :
>And when my uncle told me so, he wept,
>And hugg'd me in his arm, and kindly kiss'd my cheek;
>Bade me rely on him as on my father,
>And he would love me dearly as his child.

DUCHESS OF YORK
>Oh, that deceit should steal such gentle shapes,
>And with a virtuous vizard hide foul guile!
>He is my son; yea, and therein my shame;
>Yet from my dugs he drew not this deceit.

Boy
>Think you my uncle did dissemble, grandam?

DUCHESS OF YORK
>Ay, boy.

Boy
>I cannot think it. Hark! what noise is this?

>>*Enter QUEEN ELIZABETH, with her hair about her ears;*
>>*RIVERS, and DORSET after her*

QUEEN ELIZABETH
>Oh, who shall hinder me to wail and weep,
>To chide my fortune, and torment myself?
>I'll join with black despair against my soul,
>And to myself become an enemy.

DUCHESS OF YORK
>What means this scene of rude impatience?

QUEEN ELIZABETH
>To make an act of tragic violence:
>Edward, my lord, your son, our king, is dead.
>Why grow the branches now the root is wither'd?
>Why wither not the leaves the sap being gone?

The Tragedy of Richard the Third — Act II

    If you will live, lament; if die, be brief,
    That our swift-winged souls may catch the king's;
    Or, like obedient subjects, follow him
    To his new kingdom of perpetual rest.
DUCHESS OF YORK
    Ah, so much interest have I in thy sorrow
    As I had title in thy noble husband!
    I have bewept a worthy husband's death,
    And lived by looking on his images:
    But now two mirrors of his princely semblance
    Are crack'd in pieces by malignant death,
    And I for comfort have but one false glass,
    Which grieves me when I see my shame in him.
    Thou art a widow; yet thou art a mother,
    And hast the comfort of thy children left thee:
    But death hath snatch'd my husband from mine arms,
    And pluck'd two crutches from my feeble limbs,
    Edward and Clarence. O, what cause have I,
    Thine being but a moiety of my grief,
    To overgo thy plaints and drown thy cries!
Boy
    Good aunt, you wept not for our father's death;
    How can we aid you with our kindred tears?
Girl
    Our fatherless distress was left unmoan'd;
    Your widow-dolour likewise be unwept!
QUEEN ELIZABETH
    Give me no help in lamentation;
    I am not barren to bring forth complaints
    All springs reduce their currents to mine eyes,
    That I, being govern'd by the watery moon,
    May send forth plenteous tears to drown the world!
    Oh for my husband, for my dear lord Edward!

Children
   Oh for our father, for our dear lord Clarence!
DUCHESS OF YORK
   Alas for both, both mine, Edward and Clarence!
QUEEN ELIZABETH
   What stay had I but Edward? and he's gone.
Children
   What stay had we but Clarence? and he's gone.
DUCHESS OF YORK
   What stays had I but they? and they are gone.
QUEEN ELIZABETH
   Was never widow had so dear a loss!
Children
   Were never orphans had so dear a loss!
DUCHESS OF YORK
   Was never mother had so dear a loss!
   Alas, I am the mother of these moans!
   Their woes are parcell'd, mine are general.
   She for an Edward weeps, and so do I;
   I for a Clarence weep, so doth not she:
   These babes for Clarence weep and so do I;
   I for an Edward weep, so do not they:
   Alas, you three, on me, threefold distress'd,
   Pour all your tears! I am your sorrow's nurse,
   And I will pamper it with lamentations.
DORSET
   Comfort, dear mother: God is much displeased
   That you take with unthankfulness, his doing:
   In common worldly things, 'tis call'd ungrateful,
   With dull unwilligness to repay a debt
   Which with a bounteous hand was kindly lent;
   Much more to be thus opposite with heaven,
   For it requires the royal debt it lent you.

The Tragedy of Richard the Third — Act II

RIVERS
    Madam, bethink you, like a careful mother,
    Of the young prince your son: send straight for him
    Let him be crown'd; in him your comfort lives:
    Drown desperate sorrow in dead Edward's grave,
    And plant your joys in living Edward's throne.

Enter GLOUCESTER, BUCKINGHAM, DERBY, HASTINGS, and RATCLIFF

GLOUCESTER
    Madam, have comfort: all of us have cause
    To wail the dimming of our shining star;
    But none can cure their harms by wailing them.
    Madam, my mother, I do cry you mercy;
    I did not see your grace: humbly on my knee
    I crave your blessing.
DUCHESS OF YORK
    God bless thee; and put meekness in thy mind,
    Love, charity, obedience, and true duty!
GLOUCESTER
        [Aside]
    Amen; and make me die a good old man!
    That is the butt-end of a mother's blessing:
    I marvel why her grace did leave it out.
BUCKINGHAM
    You cloudy princes and heart-sorrowing peers,
    That bear this mutual heavy load of moan,
    Now cheer each other in each other's love
    Though we have spent our harvest of this king,
    We are to reap the harvest of his son.
    The broken rancour of your high-swoln hearts,
    But lately splinter'd, knit, and join'd together,
    Must gently be preserved, cherish'd, and kept:
    Me seemeth good, that, with some little train,

The Tragedy of Richard the Third — Act II

    Forthwith from Ludlow the young prince be fetch'd
    Hither to London, to be crown'd our king.
RIVERS
    Why with some little train, my Lord of Buckingham?
BUCKINGHAM
    Marry, my lord, lest, by a multitude,
    The new-heal'd wound of malice should break out,
    Which would be so much the more dangerous
    By how much the estate is green and yet ungovern'd:
    Where every horse bears his commanding rein,
    And may direct his course as please himself,
    As well the fear of harm, as harm apparent,
    In my opinion, ought to be prevented.
GLOUCESTER
    I hope the king made peace with all of us
    And the compact is firm and true in me.
RIVERS
    And so in me; and so, I think, in all:
    Yet, since it is but green, it should be put
    To no apparent likelihood of breach,
    Which haply by much company might be urged:
    Therefore I say with noble Buckingham,
    That it is meet so few should fetch the prince.
HASTINGS
    And so say I.
GLOUCESTER
    Then be it so; and go we to determine
    Who they shall be that straight shall post to Ludlow.
    Madam, and you, my mother, will you go
    To give your censures in this weighty business?
QUEEN ELIZABETH DUCHESS OF YORK
    With all our harts.

*   Exeunt all but BUCKINGHAM and GLOUCESTER*

BUCKINGHAM
  My lord, whoever journeys to the Prince,
  For God's sake, let not us two be behind;
  For, by the way, I'll sort occasion,
  As index to the story we late talk'd of,
  To part the queen's proud kindred from the king.
GLOUCESTER
  My other self, my counsel's consistory,
  My oracle, my prophet! My dear cousin,
  I, like a child, will go by thy direction.
  Towards Ludlow then, for we'll not stay behind.

Exeunt

SCENE III.
London. A street.

Enter two Citizens meeting

First Citizen
  Neighbour, well met: whither away so fast?
Second Citizen
  I promise you, I scarcely know myself:
  Hear you the news abroad?
First Citizen
  Ay, that the king is dead.
Second Citizen
  Bad news, by'r lady; seldom comes the better:
  I fear, I fear 'twill prove a troublous world.

Enter another Citizen

Third Citizen
  Neighbours, God speed!

The Tragedy of Richard the Third — Act II

First Citizen
   Give you good morrow, sir.
Third Citizen
   Doth this news hold of good King Edward's death?
Second Citizen
   Ay, sir, it is too true; God help the while!
Third Citizen
   Then, masters, look to see a troublous world.
First Citizen
   No, no; by God's good grace his son shall reign.
Third Citizen
   Woe to the land that's govern'd by a child!
Second Citizen
   In him there is a hope of government,
   That in his nonage council under him,
   And in his full and ripen'd years himself,
   No doubt, shall then and till then govern well.
First Citizen
   So stood the state when Henry the Sixth
   Was crown'd in Paris but at nine months old.
Third Citizen
   Stood the state so? No, no, good friends, God wot;
   For then this land was famously enrich'd
   With politic grave counsel; then the king
   Had virtuous uncles to protect his grace.
First Citizen
   Why, so hath this, both by the father and mother.
Third Citizen
   Better it were they all came by the father,
   Or by the father there were none at all;
   For emulation now, who shall be nearest,
   Will touch us all too near, if God prevent not.
   O, full of danger is the Duke of Gloucester!
   And the queen's sons and brothers haught and proud:

The Tragedy of Richard the Third — Act II

    And were they to be ruled, and not to rule,
    This sickly land might solace as before.
First Citizen
    Come, come, we fear the worst; all shall be well.
Third Citizen
    When clouds appear, wise men put on their cloaks;
    When great leaves fall, the winter is at hand;
    When the sun sets, who doth not look for night?
    Untimely storms make men expect a dearth.
    All may be well; but, if God sort it so,
    'Tis more than we deserve, or I expect.
Second Citizen
    Truly, the souls of men are full of dread:
    Ye cannot reason almost with a man
    That looks not heavily and full of fear.
Third Citizen
    Before the times of change, still is it so:
    By a divine instinct men's minds mistrust
    Ensuing dangers; as by proof, we see
    The waters swell before a boisterous storm.
    But leave it all to God. whither away?
Second Citizen
    Marry, we were sent for to the justices.
Third Citizen
    And so was I: I'll bear you company.

                              Exeunt

The Tragedy of Richard the Third — Act II

SCENE IV.
London. The palace.

Enter the ARCHBISHOP OF YORK, young YORK, QUEEN ELIZABETH, and the DUCHESS OF YORK

ARCHBISHOP OF YORK
  Last night, I hear, they lay at Northampton;
  At Stony-Stratford will they be to-night:
  To-morrow, or next day, they will be here.
DUCHESS OF YORK
  I long with all my heart to see the prince:
  I hope he is much grown since last I saw him.
QUEEN ELIZABETH
  But I hear, no; they say my son of York
  Hath almost overta'en him in his growth.
YORK
  Ay, mother; but I would not have it so.
DUCHESS OF YORK
  Why, my young cousin, it is good to grow.
YORK
  Grandam, one night, as we did sit at supper,
  My uncle Rivers talk'd how I did grow
  More than my brother: 'Ay,' quoth my uncle Gloucester,
  'Small herbs have grace, great weeds do grow apace:'
  And since, methinks, I would not grow so fast,
  Because sweet flowers are slow and weeds make haste.
DUCHESS OF YORK
  Good faith, good faith, the saying did not hold
  In him that did object the same to thee;
  He was the wretched'st thing when he was young,
  So long a-growing and so leisurely,
  That, if this rule were true, he should be gracious.

ARCHBISHOP OF YORK
  Why, madam, so, no doubt, he is.
DUCHESS OF YORK
  I hope he is; but yet let mothers doubt.
YORK
  Now, by my troth, if I had been remember'd,
  I could have given my uncle's grace a flout,
  To touch his growth nearer than he touch'd mine.
DUCHESS OF YORK
  How, my pretty York? I pray thee, let me hear it.
YORK
  Marry, they say my uncle grew so fast
  That he could gnaw a crust at two hours old
  'Twas full two years ere I could get a tooth.
  Grandam, this would have been a biting jest.
DUCHESS OF YORK
  I pray thee, pretty York, who told thee this?
YORK
  Grandam, his nurse.
DUCHESS OF YORK
  His nurse! why, she was dead ere thou wert born.
YORK
  If 'twere not she, I cannot tell who told me.
QUEEN ELIZABETH
  A parlous boy: go to, you are too shrewd.
ARCHBISHOP OF YORK
  Good madam, be not angry with the child.
QUEEN ELIZABETH
  Pitchers have ears.

Enter a Messenger

ARCHBISHOP OF YORK
  Here comes a messenger. What news?

Messenger
  Such news, my lord, as grieves me to unfold.
QUEEN ELIZABETH
  How fares the prince?
Messenger
  Well, madam, and in health.
DUCHESS OF YORK
  What is thy news then?
Messenger
  Lord Rivers and Lord Grey are sent to Pomfret,
  With them Sir Thomas Vaughan, prisoners.
DUCHESS OF YORK
  Who hath committed them?
Messenger
  The mighty dukes
  Gloucester and Buckingham.
QUEEN ELIZABETH
  For what offence?
Messenger
  The sum of all I can, I have disclosed;
  Why or for what these nobles were committed
  Is all unknown to me, my gracious lady.
QUEEN ELIZABETH
  Ay me, I see the downfall of our house!
  The tiger now hath seized the gentle hind;
  Insulting tyranny begins to jet
  Upon the innocent and aweless throne:
  Welcome, destruction, death, and massacre!
  I see, as in a map, the end of all.
DUCHESS OF YORK
  Accursed and unquiet wrangling days,
  How many of you have mine eyes beheld!
  My husband lost his life to get the crown;
  And often up and down my sons were toss'd,

The Tragedy of Richard the Third — Act II

    For me to joy and weep their gain and loss:
    And being seated, and domestic broils
    Clean over-blown, themselves, the conquerors.
    Make war upon themselves; blood against blood,
    Self against self: O, preposterous
    And frantic outrage, end thy damned spleen;
    Or let me die, to look on death no more!
QUEEN ELIZABETH
    Come, come, my boy; we will to sanctuary.
    Madam, farewell.
DUCHESS OF YORK
    I'll go along with you.
QUEEN ELIZABETH
    You have no cause.
ARCHBISHOP OF YORK
    My gracious lady, go;
    And thither bear your treasure and your goods.
    For my part, I'll resign unto your grace
    The seal I keep: and so betide to me
    As well I tender you and all of yours!
    Come, I'll conduct you to the sanctuary.

Exeunt

ACT III

SCENE I.
London. A street.

The trumpets sound. Enter the young PRINCE EDWARD, GLOUCESTER, BUCKINGHAM, CARDINAL, CATESBY, and others

BUCKINGHAM
  Welcome, sweet prince, to London, to your chamber.
GLOUCESTER
  Welcome, dear cousin, my thoughts' sovereign
  The weary way hath made you melancholy.
PRINCE EDWARD
  No, uncle; but our crosses on the way
  Have made it tedious, wearisome, and heavy
  I want more uncles here to welcome me.
GLOUCESTER
  Sweet prince, the untainted virtue of your years
  Hath not yet dived into the world's deceit
  Nor more can you distinguish of a man
  Than of his outward show; which, God he knows,
  Seldom or never jumpeth with the heart.
  Those uncles which you want were dangerous;
  Your grace attended to their sugar'd words,
  But look'd not on the poison of their hearts :
  God keep you from them, and from such false friends!
PRINCE EDWARD
  God keep me from false friends! but they were none.
GLOUCESTER
  My lord, the mayor of London comes to greet you.

The Tragedy of Richard the Third — Act III

Enter the Lord Mayor and his train

Lord Mayor
   God bless your grace with health and happy days!
PRINCE EDWARD
   I thank you, good my lord; and thank you all.
   I thought my mother, and my brother York,
   Would long ere this have met us on the way
   Fie, what a slug is Hastings, that he comes not
   To tell us whether they will come or no!

Enter HASTINGS

BUCKINGHAM
   And, in good time, here comes the sweating lord.
PRINCE EDWARD
   Welcome, my lord: what, will our mother come?
HASTINGS
   On what occasion, God he knows, not I,
   The queen your mother, and your brother York,
   Have taken sanctuary: the tender prince
   Would fain have come with me to meet your grace,
   But by his mother was perforce withheld.
BUCKINGHAM
   Fie, what an indirect and peevish course
   Is this of hers! Lord cardinal, will your grace
   Persuade the queen to send the Duke of York
   Unto his princely brother presently?
   If she deny, Lord Hastings, go with him,
   And from her jealous arms pluck him perforce.
CARDINAL
   My Lord of Buckingham, if my weak oratory
   Can from his mother win the Duke of York,
   Anon expect him here; but if she be obdurate
   To mild entreaties, God in heaven forbid

We should infringe the holy privilege
Of blessed sanctuary! not for all this land
Would I be guilty of so deep a sin.
BUCKINGHAM
You are too senseless--obstinate, my lord,
Too ceremonious and traditional
Weigh it but with the grossness of this age,
You break not sanctuary in seizing him.
The benefit thereof is always granted
To those whose dealings have deserved the place,
And those who have the wit to claim the place:
This prince hath neither claim'd it nor deserved it;
And therefore, in mine opinion, cannot have it:
Then, taking him from thence that is not there,
You break no privilege nor charter there.
Oft have I heard of sanctuary men;
But sanctuary children ne'er till now.
CARDINAL
My lord, you shall o'er-rule my mind for once.
Come on, Lord Hastings, will you go with me?
HASTINGS
I go, my lord.
PRINCE EDWARD
Good lords, make all the speedy haste you may.

Exeunt CARDINAL and HASTINGS

Say, uncle Gloucester, if our brother come,
Where shall we sojourn till our coronation?
GLOUCESTER
Where it seems best unto your royal self.
If I may counsel you, some day or two
Your highness shall repose you at the Tower:
Then where you please, and shall be thought most fit
For your best health and recreation.

PRINCE EDWARD
  I do not like the Tower, of any place.
  Did Julius Caesar build that place, my lord?
BUCKINGHAM
  He did, my gracious lord, begin that place;
  Which, since, succeeding ages have re-edified.
PRINCE EDWARD
  Is it upon record, or else reported
  Successively from age to age, he built it?
BUCKINGHAM
  Upon record, my gracious lord.
PRINCE EDWARD
  But say, my lord, it were not register'd,
  Methinks the truth should live from age to age,
  As 'twere retail'd to all posterity,
  Even to the general all-ending day.
GLOUCESTER
      [Aside]
  So wise so young, they say, do never
  live long.
PRINCE EDWARD
  What say you, uncle?
GLOUCESTER
  I say, without characters, fame lives long.
      [Aside]
  Thus, like the formal vice, Iniquity,
  I moralize two meanings in one word.
PRINCE EDWARD
  That Julius Caesar was a famous man;
  With what his valour did enrich his wit,
  His wit set down to make his valour live
  Death makes no conquest of this conqueror;
  For now he lives in fame, though not in life.
  I'll tell you what, my cousin Buckingham,--

BUCKINGHAM
   What, my gracious lord?
PRINCE EDWARD
   An if I live until I be a man,
   I'll win our ancient right in France again,
   Or die a soldier, as I lived a king.
GLOUCESTER
      [Aside]
   Short summers lightly have a forward spring.

   Enter young YORK, HASTINGS, and the CARDINAL

BUCKINGHAM
   Now, in good time, here comes the Duke of York.
PRINCE EDWARD
   Richard of York! how fares our loving brother?
YORK
   Well, my dread lord; so must I call you now.
PRINCE EDWARD
   Ay, brother, to our grief, as it is yours:
   Too late he died that might have kept that title,
   Which by his death hath lost much majesty.
GLOUCESTER
   How fares our cousin, noble Lord of York?
YORK
   I thank you, gentle uncle. O, my lord,
   You said that idle weeds are fast in growth
   The prince my brother hath outgrown me far.
GLOUCESTER
   He hath, my lord.
YORK
   And therefore is he idle?
GLOUCESTER
   O, my fair cousin, I must not say so.

The Tragedy of Richard the Third — Act III

YORK
  Then is he more beholding to you than I.
GLOUCESTER
  He may command me as my sovereign;
  But you have power in me as in a kinsman.
YORK
  I pray you, uncle, give me this dagger.
GLOUCESTER
  My dagger, little cousin? with all my heart.
PRINCE EDWARD
  A beggar, brother?
YORK
  Of my kind uncle, that I know will give;
  And being but a toy, which is no grief to give.
GLOUCESTER
  A greater gift than that I'll give my cousin.
YORK
  A greater gift! O, that's the sword to it.
GLOUCESTER
  A gentle cousin, were it light enough.
YORK
  O, then, I see, you will part but with light gifts;
  In weightier things you'll say a beggar nay.
GLOUCESTER
  It is too heavy for your grace to wear.
YORK
  I weigh it lightly, were it heavier.
GLOUCESTER
  What, would you have my weapon, little lord?
YORK
  I would, that I might thank you as you call me.
GLOUCESTER
  How?

The Tragedy of Richard the Third — Act III

YORK
　Little.
PRINCE EDWARD
　My Lord of York will still be cross in talk:
　Uncle, your grace knows how to bear with him.
YORK
　You mean, to bear me, not to bear with me:
　Uncle, my brother mocks both you and me;
　Because that I am little, like an ape,
　He thinks that you should bear me on your shoulders.
BUCKINGHAM
　With what a sharp-provided wit he reasons!
　To mitigate the scorn he gives his uncle,
　He prettily and aptly taunts himself:
　So cunning and so young is wonderful.
GLOUCESTER
　My lord, will't please you pass along?
　Myself and my good cousin Buckingham
　Will to your mother, to entreat of her
　To meet you at the Tower and welcome you.
YORK
　What, will you go unto the Tower, my lord?
PRINCE EDWARD
　My lord protector needs will have it so.
YORK
　I shall not sleep in quiet at the Tower.
GLOUCESTER
　Why, what should you fear?
YORK
　Marry, my uncle Clarence' angry ghost:
　My grandam told me he was murdered there.
PRINCE EDWARD
　I fear no uncles dead.

The Tragedy of Richard the Third — Act III

GLOUCESTER
  Nor none that live, I hope.
PRINCE EDWARD
  An if they live, I hope I need not fear.
  But come, my lord; and with a heavy heart,
  Thinking on them, go I unto the Tower.

  A Sennet. Exeunt all but GLOUCESTER, BUCKINGHAM and CATESBY

BUCKINGHAM
  Think you, my lord, this little prating York
  Was not incensed by his subtle mother
  To taunt and scorn you thus opprobriously?
GLOUCESTER
  No doubt, no doubt; O, 'tis a parlous boy;
  Bold, quick, ingenious, forward, capable
  He is all the mother's, from the top to toe.
BUCKINGHAM
  Well, let them rest. Come hither, Catesby.
  Thou art sworn as deeply to effect what we intend
  As closely to conceal what we impart:
  Thou know'st our reasons urged upon the way;
  What think'st thou? is it not an easy matter
  To make William Lord Hastings of our mind,
  For the instalment of this noble duke
  In the seat royal of this famous isle?
CATESBY
  He for his father's sake so loves the prince,
  That he will not be won to aught against him.
BUCKINGHAM
  What think'st thou, then, of Stanley? what will he?
CATESBY
  He will do all in all as Hastings doth.

The Tragedy of Richard the Third — Act III

BUCKINGHAM
 Well, then, no more but this: go, gentle Catesby,
 And, as it were far off sound thou Lord Hastings,
 How doth he stand affected to our purpose;
 And summon him to-morrow to the Tower,
 To sit about the coronation.
 If thou dost find him tractable to us,
 Encourage him, and show him all our reasons:
 If he be leaden, icy-cold, unwilling,
 Be thou so too; and so break off your talk,
 And give us notice of his inclination:
 For we to-morrow hold divided councils,
 Wherein thyself shalt highly be employ'd.
GLOUCESTER
 Commend me to Lord William: tell him, Catesby,
 His ancient knot of dangerous adversaries
 To-morrow are let blood at Pomfret-castle;
 And bid my friend, for joy of this good news,
 Give mistress Shore one gentle kiss the more.
BUCKINGHAM
 Good Catesby, go, effect this business soundly.
CATESBY
 My good lords both, with all the heed I may.
GLOUCESTER
 Shall we hear from you, Catesby, ere we sleep?
CATESBY
 You shall, my lord.
GLOUCESTER
 At Crosby Place, there shall you find us both.

      Exit CATESBY

BUCKINGHAM
 Now, my lord, what shall we do, if we perceive
 Lord Hastings will not yield to our complots?

The Tragedy of Richard the Third — Act III

GLOUCESTER
   Chop off his head, man; somewhat we will do:
   And, look, when I am king, claim thou of me
   The earldom of Hereford, and the moveables
   Whereof the king my brother stood possess'd.
BUCKINGHAM
   I'll claim that promise at your grace's hands.
GLOUCESTER
   And look to have it yielded with all willingness.
   Come, let us sup betimes, that afterwards
   We may digest our complots in some form.

Exeunt

SCENE II.
Before Lord Hastings' house.

Enter a Messenger

Messenger
   What, ho! my lord!
HASTINGS
         [Within]
Who knocks at the door?
Messenger
   A messenger from the Lord Stanley.

Enter HASTINGS

HASTINGS
   What is't o'clock?
Messenger
   Upon the stroke of four.
HASTINGS
   Cannot thy master sleep these tedious nights?

The Tragedy of Richard the Third — Act III

Messenger
   So it should seem by that I have to say.
   First, he commends him to your noble lordship.
HASTINGS
   And then?
Messenger
   And then he sends you word
   He dreamt to-night the boar had razed his helm:
   Besides, he says there are two councils held;
   And that may be determined at the one
   which may make you and him to rue at the other.
   Therefore he sends to know your lordship's pleasure,
   If presently you will take horse with him,
   And with all speed post with him toward the north,
   To shun the danger that his soul divines.
HASTINGS
   Go, fellow, go, return unto thy lord;
   Bid him not fear the separated councils
   His honour and myself are at the one,
   And at the other is my servant Catesby
   Where nothing can proceed that toucheth us
   Whereof I shall not have intelligence.
   Tell him his fears are shallow, wanting instance:
   And for his dreams, I wonder he is so fond
   To trust the mockery of unquiet slumbers
   To fly the boar before the boar pursues,
   Were to incense the boar to follow us
   And make pursuit where he did mean no chase.
   Go, bid thy master rise and come to me
   And we will both together to the Tower,
   Where, he shall see, the boar will use us kindly.
Messenger
   My gracious lord, I'll tell him what you say.

Exit

The Tragedy of Richard the Third — Act III

Enter CATESBY

CATESBY
  Many good morrows to my noble lord!
HASTINGS
  Good morrow, Catesby; you are early stirring
  What news, what news, in this our tottering state?
CATESBY
  It is a reeling world, indeed, my lord;
  And I believe twill never stand upright
  Till Richard wear the garland of the realm.
HASTINGS
  How! wear the garland! dost thou mean the crown?
CATESBY
  Ay, my good lord.
HASTINGS
  I'll have this crown of mine cut from my shoulders
  Ere I will see the crown so foul misplaced.
  But canst thou guess that he doth aim at it?
CATESBY
  Ay, on my life; and hopes to find forward
  Upon his party for the gain thereof:
  And thereupon he sends you this good news,
  That this same very day your enemies,
  The kindred of the queen, must die at Pomfret.
HASTINGS
  Indeed, I am no mourner for that news,
  Because they have been still mine enemies:
  But, that I'll give my voice on Richard's side,
  To bar my master's heirs in true descent,
  God knows I will not do it, to the death.
CATESBY
  God keep your lordship in that gracious mind!

The Tragedy of Richard the Third — Act III

HASTINGS
   But I shall laugh at this a twelve-month hence,
   That they who brought me in my master's hate
   I live to look upon their tragedy.
   I tell thee, Catesby--
CATESBY
   What, my lord?
HASTINGS
   Ere a fortnight make me elder,
   I'll send some packing that yet think not on it.
CATESBY
   'Tis a vile thing to die, my gracious lord,
   When men are unprepared and look not for it.
HASTINGS
   O monstrous, monstrous! and so falls it out
   With Rivers, Vaughan, Grey: and so 'twill do
   With some men else, who think themselves as safe
   As thou and I; who, as thou know'st, are dear
   To princely Richard and to Buckingham.
CATESBY
   The princes both make high account of you;
        Aside
   For they account his head upon the bridge.
HASTINGS
   I know they do; and I have well deserved it.

        Enter STANLEY

   Come on, come on; where is your boar-spear, man?
   Fear you the boar, and go so unprovided?

STANLEY
   My lord, good morrow; good morrow, Catesby:
   You may jest on, but, by the holy rood,
   I do not like these several councils, I.

The Tragedy of Richard the Third — Act III

HASTINGS
   My lord,
   I hold my life as dear as you do yours;
   And never in my life, I do protest,
   Was it more precious to me than 'tis now:
   Think you, but that I know our state secure,
   I would be so triumphant as I am?
STANLEY
   The lords at Pomfret, when they rode from London,
   Were jocund, and supposed their state was sure,
   And they indeed had no cause to mistrust;
   But yet, you see how soon the day o'ercast.
   This sudden stag of rancour I misdoubt:
   Pray God, I say, I prove a needless coward!
   What, shall we toward the Tower? the day is spent.
HASTINGS
   Come, come, have with you. Wot you what, my lord?
   To-day the lords you talk of are beheaded.
LORD STANLEY
   They, for their truth, might better wear their heads
   Than some that have accused them wear their hats.
   But come, my lord, let us away.

Enter a Pursuivant

HASTINGS
   Go on before; I'll talk with this good fellow.

Exeunt STANLEY and CATESBY

   How now, sirrah! how goes the world with thee?
Pursuivant
   The better that your lordship please to ask.
HASTINGS
   I tell thee, man, 'tis better with me now

The Tragedy of Richard the Third — Act III

Than when I met thee last where now we meet:
Then was I going prisoner to the Tower,
By the suggestion of the queen's allies;
But now, I tell thee--keep it to thyself--
This day those enemies are put to death,
And I in better state than e'er I was.

Pursuivant
God hold it, to your honour's good content!

HASTINGS
Gramercy, fellow: there, drink that for me.

Throws him his purse

Pursuivant
God save your lordship!

Exit

Enter a Priest

Priest
Well met, my lord; I am glad to see your honour.

HASTINGS
I thank thee, good Sir John, with all my heart.
I am in your debt for your last exercise;
Come the next Sabbath, and I will content you.

He whispers in his ear

Enter BUCKINGHAM

BUCKINGHAM
What, talking with a priest, lord chamberlain?
Your friends at Pomfret, they do need the priest;
Your honour hath no shriving work in hand.

HASTINGS
  Good faith, and when I met this holy man,
  Those men you talk of came into my mind.
  What, go you toward the Tower?
BUCKINGHAM
  I do, my lord; but long I shall not stay
  I shall return before your lordship thence.
HASTINGS
  'Tis like enough, for I stay dinner there.
BUCKINGHAM
            [Aside]
  And supper too, although thou know'st it not.
  Come, will you go?
HASTINGS
  I'll wait upon your lordship.

                    Exeunt

SCENE III.
Pomfret Castle.

Enter RATCLIFF, with halberds, carrying RIVERS, GREY, and VAUGHAN to death

RATCLIFF
  Come, bring forth the prisoners.
RIVERS
  Sir Richard Ratcliff, let me tell thee this:
  To-day shalt thou behold a subject die
  For truth, for duty, and for loyalty.
GREY
  God keep the prince from all the pack of you!
  A knot you are of damned blood-suckers!

The Tragedy of Richard the Third — Act III

VAUGHAN
   You live that shall cry woe for this after.
RATCLIFF
   Dispatch; the limit of your lives is out.
RIVERS
   O Pomfret, Pomfret! O thou bloody prison,
   Fatal and ominous to noble peers!
   Within the guilty closure of thy walls
   Richard the second here was hack'd to death;
   And, for more slander to thy dismal seat,
   We give thee up our guiltless blood to drink.
GREY
   Now Margaret's curse is fall'n upon our heads,
   For standing by when Richard stabb'd her son.
RIVERS
   Then cursed she Hastings, then cursed she Buckingham,
   Then cursed she Richard. O, remember, God
   To hear her prayers for them, as now for us
   And for my sister and her princely sons,
   Be satisfied, dear God, with our true blood,
   Which, as thou know'st, unjustly must be spilt.
RATCLIFF
   Make haste; the hour of death is expiate.
RIVERS
   Come, Grey, come, Vaughan, let us all embrace:
   And take our leave, until we meet in heaven.

Exeunt

The Tragedy of Richard the Third — Act III

SCENE IV.
The Tower of London.

Enter BUCKINGHAM, DERBY, HASTINGS, the BISHOP OF ELY, RATCLIFF, LOVEL, with others, and take their seats at a table

HASTINGS
   My lords, at once: the cause why we are met
   Is, to determine of the coronation.
   In God's name, speak: when is the royal day?
BUCKINGHAM
   Are all things fitting for that royal time?
DERBY
   It is, and wants but nomination.
BISHOP OF ELY
   To-morrow, then, I judge a happy day.
BUCKINGHAM
   Who knows the lord protector's mind herein?
   Who is most inward with the royal duke?
BISHOP OF ELY
   Your grace, we think, should soonest know his mind.
BUCKINGHAM
   Who, I, my lord I we know each other's faces,
   But for our hearts, he knows no more of mine,
   Than I of yours;
   Nor I no more of his, than you of mine.
   Lord Hastings, you and he are near in love.
HASTINGS
   I thank his grace, I know he loves me well;
   But, for his purpose in the coronation.
   I have not sounded him, nor he deliver'd
   His gracious pleasure any way therein:
   But you, my noble lords, may name the time;
   And in the duke's behalf I'll give my voice,

The Tragedy of Richard the Third — Act III

Which, I presume, he'll take in gentle part.

Enter GLOUCESTER

BISHOP OF ELY
  Now in good time, here comes the duke himself.
GLOUCESTER
  My noble lords and cousins all, good morrow.
  I have been long a sleeper; but, I hope,
  My absence doth neglect no great designs,
  Which by my presence might have been concluded.
BUCKINGHAM
  Had not you come upon your cue, my lord
  William Lord Hastings had pronounced your part,--
  I mean, your voice,--for crowning of the king.
GLOUCESTER
  Than my Lord Hastings no man might be bolder;
  His lordship knows me well, and loves me well.
HASTINGS
  I thank your grace.
GLOUCESTER
  My lord of Ely!
BISHOP OF ELY
  My lord?
GLOUCESTER
  When I was last in Holborn,
  I saw good strawberries in your garden there
  I do beseech you send for some of them.
BISHOP OF ELY
  Marry, and will, my lord, with all my heart.

Exit

GLOUCESTER
  Cousin of Buckingham, a word with you.

The Tragedy of Richard the Third — Act III

Drawing him aside

Catesby hath sounded Hastings in our business,
And finds the testy gentleman so hot,
As he will lose his head ere give consent
His master's son, as worshipful as he terms it,
Shall lose the royalty of England's throne.
BUCKINGHAM
Withdraw you hence, my lord, I'll follow you.

Exit GLOUCESTER, BUCKINGHAM following

DERBY
We have not yet set down this day of triumph.
To-morrow, in mine opinion, is too sudden;
For I myself am not so well provided
As else I would be, were the day prolong'd.

Re-enter BISHOP OF ELY

BISHOP OF ELY
Where is my lord protector? I have sent for these strawberries.
HASTINGS
His grace looks cheerfully and smooth to-day;
There's some conceit or other likes him well,
When he doth bid good morrow with such a spirit.
I think there's never a man in Christendom
That can less hide his love or hate than he;
For by his face straight shall you know his heart.
DERBY
What of his heart perceive you in his face
By any likelihood he show'd to-day?
HASTINGS
Marry, that with no man here he is offended;

For, were he, he had shown it in his looks.
DERBY
I pray God he be not, I say.

Re-enter GLOUCESTER and BUCKINGHAM

GLOUCESTER
I pray you all, tell me what they deserve
That do conspire my death with devilish plots
Of damned witchcraft, and that have prevail'd
Upon my body with their hellish charms?
HASTINGS
The tender love I bear your grace, my lord,
Makes me most forward in this noble presence
To doom the offenders, whatsoever they be
I say, my lord, they have deserved death.
GLOUCESTER
Then be your eyes the witness of this ill:
See how I am bewitch'd; behold mine arm
Is, like a blasted sapling, wither'd up:
And this is Edward's wife, that monstrous witch,
Consorted with that harlot strumpet Shore,
That by their witchcraft thus have marked me.
HASTINGS
If they have done this thing, my gracious lord--
GLOUCESTER
If I thou protector of this damned strumpet--
Tellest thou me of 'ifs'? Thou art a traitor:
Off with his head! Now, by Saint Paul I swear,
I will not dine until I see the same.
Lovel and Ratcliff, look that it be done:
The rest, that love me, rise and follow me.

Exeunt all but HASTINGS, RATCLIFF, and LOVEL

The Tragedy of Richard the Third — Act III

HASTINGS
  Woe, woe for England! not a whit for me;
  For I, too fond, might have prevented this.
  Stanley did dream the boar did raze his helm;
  But I disdain'd it, and did scorn to fly:
  Three times to-day my foot-cloth horse did stumble,
  And startled, when he look'd upon the Tower,
  As loath to bear me to the slaughter-house.
  O, now I want the priest that spake to me:
  I now repent I told the pursuivant
  As 'twere triumphing at mine enemies,
  How they at Pomfret bloodily were butcher'd,
  And I myself secure in grace and favour.
  O Margaret, Margaret, now thy heavy curse
  Is lighted on poor Hastings' wretched head!
RATCLIFF
  Dispatch, my lord; the duke would be at dinner:
  Make a short shrift; he longs to see your head.
HASTINGS
  O momentary grace of mortal men,
  Which we more hunt for than the grace of God!
  Who builds his hopes in air of your good looks,
  Lives like a drunken sailor on a mast,
  Ready, with every nod, to tumble down
  Into the fatal bowels of the deep.
LOVEL
  Come, come, dispatch; 'tis bootless to exclaim.
HASTINGS
  O bloody Richard! miserable England!
  I prophesy the fearful'st time to thee
  That ever wretched age hath look'd upon.
  Come, lead me to the block; bear him my head.
  They smile at me that shortly shall be dead.

Exeunt

The Tragedy of Richard the Third — Act III

SCENE V.
The Tower-walls.

Enter GLOUCESTER and BUCKINGHAM, in rotten armour, marvellous ill-favoured

GLOUCESTER
  Come, cousin, canst thou quake, and change thy colour,
  Murder thy breath in the middle of a word,
  And then begin again, and stop again,
  As if thou wert distraught and mad with terror?
BUCKINGHAM
  Tut, I can counterfeit the deep tragedian;
  Speak and look back, and pry on every side,
  Tremble and start at wagging of a straw,
  Intending deep suspicion: ghastly looks
  Are at my service, like enforced smiles;
  And both are ready in their offices,
  At any time, to grace my stratagems.
  But what, is Catesby gone?
GLOUCESTER
  He is; and, see, he brings the mayor along.

Enter the Lord Mayor and CATESBY

BUCKINGHAM
  Lord mayor,--
GLOUCESTER
  Look to the drawbridge there!
BUCKINGHAM
  Hark! a drum.
GLOUCESTER
  Catesby, o'erlook the walls.
BUCKINGHAM
  Lord mayor, the reason we have sent--

The Tragedy of Richard the Third — Act III

GLOUCESTER
  Look back, defend thee, here are enemies.
BUCKINGHAM
  God and our innocency defend and guard us!
GLOUCESTER
  Be patient, they are friends, Ratcliff and Lovel.

   Enter LOVEL and RATCLIFF, with HASTINGS' head

LOVEL
  Here is the head of that ignoble traitor,
  The dangerous and unsuspected Hastings.
GLOUCESTER
  So dear I loved the man, that I must weep.
  I took him for the plainest harmless creature
  That breathed upon this earth a Christian;
  Made him my book wherein my soul recorded
  The history of all her secret thoughts:
  So smooth he daub'd his vice with show of virtue,
  That, his apparent open guilt omitted,
  I mean, his conversation with Shore's wife,
  He lived from all attainder of suspect.
BUCKINGHAM
  Well, well, he was the covert'st shelter'd traitor
  That ever lived.
  Would you imagine, or almost believe,
  Were't not that, by great preservation,
  We live to tell it you, the subtle traitor
  This day had plotted, in the council-house
  To murder me and my good Lord of Gloucester?
Lord Mayor
  What, had he so?
GLOUCESTER
  What, think You we are Turks or infidels?
  Or that we would, against the form of law,

The Tragedy of Richard the Third — Act III

    Proceed thus rashly to the villain's death,
    But that the extreme peril of the case,
    The peace of England and our persons' safety,
    Enforced us to this execution?
Lord Mayor
    Now, fair befall you! he deserved his death;
    And you my good lords, both have well proceeded,
    To warn false traitors from the like attempts.
    I never look'd for better at his hands,
    After he once fell in with Mistress Shore.
GLOUCESTER
    Yet had not we determined he should die,
    Until your lordship came to see his death;
    Which now the loving haste of these our friends,
    Somewhat against our meaning, have prevented:
    Because, my lord, we would have had you heard
    The traitor speak, and timorously confess
    The manner and the purpose of his treason;
    That you might well have signified the same
    Unto the citizens, who haply may
    Misconstrue us in him and wail his death.
Lord Mayor
    But, my good lord, your grace's word shall serve,
    As well as I had seen and heard him speak
    And doubt you not, right noble princes both,
    But I'll acquaint our duteous citizens
    With all your just proceedings in this cause.
GLOUCESTER
    And to that end we wish'd your lord-ship here,
    To avoid the carping censures of the world.
BUCKINGHAM
    But since you come too late of our intents,
    Yet witness what you hear we did intend:
    And so, my good lord mayor, we bid farewell.

The Tragedy of Richard the Third — Act III

Exit Lord Mayor

GLOUCESTER
    Go, after, after, cousin Buckingham.
    The mayor towards Guildhall hies him in all post:
    There, at your meet'st advantage of the time,
    Infer the bastardy of Edward's children:
    Tell them how Edward put to death a citizen,
    Only for saying he would make his son
    Heir to the crown; meaning indeed his house,
    Which, by the sign thereof was termed so.
    Moreover, urge his hateful luxury
    And bestial appetite in change of lust;
    Which stretched to their servants, daughters, wives,
    Even where his lustful eye or savage heart,
    Without control, listed to make his prey.
    Nay, for a need, thus far come near my person:
    Tell them, when that my mother went with child
    Of that unsatiate Edward, noble York
    My princely father then had wars in France
    And, by just computation of the time,
    Found that the issue was not his begot;
    Which well appeared in his lineaments,
    Being nothing like the noble duke my father:
    But touch this sparingly, as 'twere far off,
    Because you know, my lord, my mother lives.
BUCKINGHAM
    Fear not, my lord, I'll play the orator
    As if the golden fee for which I plead
    Were for myself: and so, my lord, adieu.
GLOUCESTER
    If you thrive well, bring them to Baynard's Castle;
    Where you shall find me well accompanied
    With reverend fathers and well-learned bishops.

The Tragedy of Richard the Third — Act III

BUCKINGHAM
I go: and towards three or four o'clock
Look for the news that the Guildhall affords.

Exit BUCKINGHAM

GLOUCESTER
Go, Lovel, with all speed to Doctor Shaw;

To CATESBY

Go thou to Friar Penker; bid them both
Meet me within this hour at Baynard's Castle.

Exeunt all but GLOUCESTER

Now will I in, to take some privy order,
To draw the brats of Clarence out of sight;
And to give notice, that no manner of person
At any time have recourse unto the princes.

Exit

SCENE VI.
The same.

Enter a Scrivener, with a paper in his hand

Scrivener
This is the indictment of the good Lord Hastings;
Which in a set hand fairly is engross'd,
That it may be this day read over in Paul's.
And mark how well the sequel hangs together:
Eleven hours I spent to write it over,
For yesternight by Catesby was it brought me;
The precedent was full as long a-doing:

And yet within these five hours lived Lord Hastings,
Untainted, unexamined, free, at liberty
Here's a good world the while! Why who's so gross,
That seeth not this palpable device?
Yet who's so blind, but says he sees it not?
Bad is the world; and all will come to nought,
When such bad dealings must be seen in thought.

Exit

SCENE VII.
Baynard's Castle.

Enter GLOUCESTER and BUCKINGHAM, at several doors

GLOUCESTER
How now, my lord, what say the citizens?
BUCKINGHAM
Now, by the holy mother of our Lord,
The citizens are mum and speak not a word.
GLOUCESTER
Touch'd you the bastardy of Edward's children?
BUCKINGHAM
I did; with his contract with Lady Lucy,
And his contract by deputy in France;
The insatiate greediness of his desires,
And his enforcement of the city wives;
His tyranny for trifles; his own bastardy,
As being got, your father then in France,
His resemblance, being not like the duke;
Withal I did infer your lineaments,
Being the right idea of your father,
Both in your form and nobleness of mind;
Laid open all your victories in Scotland,

Your dicipline in war, wisdom in peace,
Your bounty, virtue, fair humility:
Indeed, left nothing fitting for the purpose
Untouch'd, or slightly handled, in discourse
And when mine oratory grew to an end
I bid them that did love their country's good
Cry 'God save Richard, England's royal king!'
GLOUCESTER
Ah! and did they so?
BUCKINGHAM
No, so God help me, they spake not a word;
But, like dumb statues or breathing stones,
Gazed each on other, and look'd deadly pale.
Which when I saw, I reprehended them;
And ask'd the mayor what meant this wilful silence:
His answer was, the people were not wont
To be spoke to but by the recorder.
Then he was urged to tell my tale again,
'Thus saith the duke, thus hath the duke inferr'd;'
But nothing spake in warrant from himself.
When he had done, some followers of mine own,
At the lower end of the hall, hurl'd up their caps,
And some ten voices cried 'God save King Richard!'
And thus I took the vantage of those few,
'Thanks, gentle citizens and friends,' quoth I;
'This general applause and loving shout
Argues your wisdoms and your love to Richard:'
And even here brake off, and came away.
GLOUCESTER
What tongueless blocks were they! would not they speak?
BUCKINGHAM
No, by my troth, my lord.
GLOUCESTER
Will not the mayor then and his brethren come?

The Tragedy of Richard the Third — Act III

BUCKINGHAM
    The mayor is here at hand: intend some fear;
    Be not you spoke with, but by mighty suit:
    And look you get a prayer-book in your hand,
    And stand betwixt two churchmen, good my lord;
    For on that ground I'll build a holy descant:
    And be not easily won to our request:
    Play the maid's part, still answer nay, and take it.
GLOUCESTER
    I go; and if you plead as well for them
    As I can say nay to thee for myself,
    No doubt well bring it to a happy issue.
BUCKINGHAM
    Go, go, up to the leads; the lord mayor knocks.

Exit GLOUCESTER

Enter the Lord Mayor and Citizens

    Welcome my lord; I dance attendance here;
    I think the duke will not be spoke withal.

Enter CATESBY

    Here comes his servant: how now, Catesby,
    What says he?
CATESBY
    My lord: he doth entreat your grace;
    To visit him to-morrow or next day:
    He is within, with two right reverend fathers,
    Divinely bent to meditation;
    And no worldly suit would he be moved,
    To draw him from his holy exercise.
BUCKINGHAM
    Return, good Catesby, to thy lord again;

Tell him, myself, the mayor and citizens,
In deep designs and matters of great moment,
No less importing than our general good,
Are come to have some conference with his grace.
CATESBY
I'll tell him what you say, my lord.

Exit

BUCKINGHAM
Ah, ha, my lord, this prince is not an Edward!
He is not lolling on a lewd day-bed,
But on his knees at meditation;
Not dallying with a brace of courtezans,
But meditating with two deep divines;
Not sleeping, to engross his idle body,
But praying, to enrich his watchful soul:
Happy were England, would this gracious prince
Take on himself the sovereignty thereof:
But, sure, I fear, we shall ne'er win him to it.
Lord Mayor
Marry, God forbid his grace should say us nay!
BUCKINGHAM
I fear he will.

Re-enter CATESBY

How now, Catesby, what says your lord?
CATESBY
My lord,
He wonders to what end you have assembled
Such troops of citizens to speak with him,
His grace not being warn'd thereof before:
My lord, he fears you mean no good to him.

The Tragedy of Richard the Third — Act III

BUCKINGHAM
>Sorry I am my noble cousin should
>Suspect me, that I mean no good to him:
>By heaven, I come in perfect love to him;
>And so once more return and tell his grace.

>>*Exit CATESBY*

>When holy and devout religious men
>Are at their beads, 'tis hard to draw them thence,
>So sweet is zealous contemplation.

>>*Enter GLOUCESTER aloft, between two Bishops. CATESBY returns*

Lord Mayor
>See, where he stands between two clergymen!

BUCKINGHAM
>Two props of virtue for a Christian prince,
>To stay him from the fall of vanity:
>And, see, a book of prayer in his hand,
>True ornaments to know a holy man.
>Famous Plantagenet, most gracious prince,
>Lend favourable ears to our request;
>And pardon us the interruption
>Of thy devotion and right Christian zeal.

GLOUCESTER
>My lord, there needs no such apology:
>I rather do beseech you pardon me,
>Who, earnest in the service of my God,
>Neglect the visitation of my friends.
>But, leaving this, what is your grace's pleasure?

BUCKINGHAM
>Even that, I hope, which pleaseth God above,
>And all good men of this ungovern'd isle.

GLOUCESTER
    I do suspect I have done some offence
    That seems disgracious in the city's eyes,
    And that you come to reprehend my ignorance.
BUCKINGHAM
    You have, my lord: would it might please your grace,
    At our entreaties, to amend that fault!
GLOUCESTER
    Else wherefore breathe I in a Christian land?
BUCKINGHAM
    Then know, it is your fault that you resign
    The supreme seat, the throne majestical,
    The scepter'd office of your ancestors,
    Your state of fortune and your due of birth,
    The lineal glory of your royal house,
    To the corruption of a blemished stock:
    Whilst, in the mildness of your sleepy thoughts,
    Which here we waken to our country's good,
    This noble isle doth want her proper limbs;
    Her face defaced with scars of infamy,
    Her royal stock graft with ignoble plants,
    And almost shoulder'd in the swallowing gulf
    Of blind forgetfulness and dark oblivion.
    Which to recure, we heartily solicit
    Your gracious self to take on you the charge
    And kingly government of this your land,
    Not as protector, steward, substitute,
    Or lowly factor for another's gain;
    But as successively from blood to blood,
    Your right of birth, your empery, your own.
    For this, consorted with the citizens,
    Your very worshipful and loving friends,
    And by their vehement instigation,
    In this just suit come I to move your grace.

The Tragedy of Richard the Third — Act III

GLOUCESTER
    I know not whether to depart in silence,
    Or bitterly to speak in your reproof.
    Best fitteth my degree or your condition
    If not to answer, you might haply think
    Tongue-tied ambition, not replying, yielded
    To bear the golden yoke of sovereignty,
    Which fondly you would here impose on me;
    If to reprove you for this suit of yours,
    So season'd with your faithful love to me.
    Then, on the other side, I cheque'd my friends.
    Therefore, to speak, and to avoid the first,
    And then, in speaking, not to incur the last,
    Definitively thus I answer you.
    Your love deserves my thanks; but my desert
    Unmeritable shuns your high request.
    First if all obstacles were cut away,
    And that my path were even to the crown,
    As my ripe revenue and due by birth
    Yet so much is my poverty of spirit,
    So mighty and so many my defects,
    As I had rather hide me from my greatness,
    Being a bark to brook no mighty sea,
    Than in my greatness covet to be hid,
    And in the vapour of my glory smother'd.
    But, God be thank'd, there's no need of me,
    And much I need to help you, if need were;
    The royal tree hath left us royal fruit,
    Which, mellow'd by the stealing hours of time,
    Will well become the seat of majesty,
    And make, no doubt, us happy by his reign.
    On him I lay what you would lay on me,
    The right and fortune of his happy stars;
    Which God defend that I should wring from him!

BUCKINGHAM
    My lord, this argues conscience in your grace;
    But the respects thereof are nice and trivial,
    All circumstances well considered.
    You say that Edward is your brother's son:
    So say we too, but not by Edward's wife;
    For first he was contract to Lady Lucy--
    Your mother lives a witness to that vow--
    And afterward by substitute betroth'd
    To Bona, sister to the King of France.
    These both put by a poor petitioner,
    A care-crazed mother of a many children,
    A beauty-waning and distressed widow,
    Even in the afternoon of her best days,
    Made prize and purchase of his lustful eye,
    Seduced the pitch and height of all his thoughts
    To base declension and loathed bigamy
    By her, in his unlawful bed, he got
    This Edward, whom our manners term the prince.
    More bitterly could I expostulate,
    Save that, for reverence to some alive,
    I give a sparing limit to my tongue.
    Then, good my lord, take to your royal self
    This proffer'd benefit of dignity;
    If non to bless us and the land withal,
    Yet to draw forth your noble ancestry
    From the corruption of abusing times,
    Unto a lineal true-derived course.
Lord Mayor
    Do, good my lord, your citizens entreat you.
BUCKINGHAM
    Refuse not, mighty lord, this proffer'd love.
CATESBY
    O, make them joyful, grant their lawful suit!

The Tragedy of Richard the Third — Act III

GLOUCESTER
  Alas, why would you heap these cares on me?
  I am unfit for state and majesty;
  I do beseech you, take it not amiss;
  I cannot nor I will not yield to you.
BUCKINGHAM
  If you refuse it,--as, in love and zeal,
  Loath to depose the child, Your brother's son;
  As well we know your tenderness of heart
  And gentle, kind, effeminate remorse,
  Which we have noted in you to your kin,
  And egally indeed to all estates,--
  Yet whether you accept our suit or no,
  Your brother's son shall never reign our king;
  But we will plant some other in the throne,
  To the disgrace and downfall of your house:
  And in this resolution here we leave you.--
  Come, citizens: 'zounds! I'll entreat no more.
GLOUCESTER
  O, do not swear, my lord of Buckingham.

       Exit BUCKINGHAM with the Citizens

CATESBY
  Call them again, my lord, and accept their suit.
ANOTHER
  Do, good my lord, lest all the land do rue it.
GLOUCESTER
  Would you enforce me to a world of care?
  Well, call them again. I am not made of stone,
  But penetrable to your. kind entreats,
  Albeit against my conscience and my soul.

       Re-enter BUCKINGHAM and the rest

The Tragedy of Richard the Third — Act III

    Cousin of Buckingham, and you sage, grave men,
    Since you will buckle fortune on my back,
    To bear her burthen, whether I will or no,
    I must have patience to endure the load:
    But if black scandal or foul-faced reproach
    Attend the sequel of your imposition,
    Your mere enforcement shall acquittance me
    From all the impure blots and stains thereof;
    For God he knows, and you may partly see,
    How far I am from the desire thereof.
Lord Mayor
    God bless your grace! we see it, and will say it.
GLOUCESTER
    In saying so, you shall but say the truth.
BUCKINGHAM
    Then I salute you with this kingly title:
    Long live Richard, England's royal king!
Lord Mayor Citizens
    Amen.
BUCKINGHAM
    To-morrow will it please you to be crown'd?
GLOUCESTER
    Even when you please, since you will have it so.
BUCKINGHAM
    To-morrow, then, we will attend your grace:
    And so most joyfully we take our leave.
GLOUCESTER
    Come, let us to our holy task again.
    Farewell, good cousin; farewell, gentle friends.

Exeunt

ACT IV

SCENE I.
Before the Tower.

Enter, on one side, QUEEN ELIZABETH, DUCHESS OF YORK, and DORSET; on the other, ANNE, Duchess of Gloucester, leading Lady Margaret Plantagenet, CLARENCE's young Daughter

DUCHESS OF YORK
  Who m eets us here? my niece Plantagenet
  Led in the hand of her kind aunt of Gloucester?
  Now, for my life, she's wandering to the Tower,
  On pure heart's love to greet the tender princes.
  Daughter, well met.
LADY ANNE
  God give your graces both
  A happy and a joyful time of day!
QUEEN ELIZABETH
  As much to you, good sister! Whither away?
LADY ANNE
  No farther than the Tower; and, as I guess,
  Upon the like devotion as yourselves,
  To gratulate the gentle princes there.
QUEEN ELIZABETH
  Kind sister, thanks: we'll enter all together.

Enter BRAKENBURY

  And, in good time, here the lieutenant comes.
  Master lieutenant, pray you, by your leave,
  How doth the prince, and my young son of York?
BRAKENBURY
  Right well, dear madam. By your patience,
  I may not suffer you to visit them;

The king hath straitly charged the contrary.
QUEEN ELIZABETH
The king! why, who's that?
BRAKENBURY
I cry you mercy: I mean the lord protector.
QUEEN ELIZABETH
The Lord protect him from that kingly title!
Hath he set bounds betwixt their love and me?
I am their mother; who should keep me from them?
DUCHESS OF YORK
I am their fathers mother; I will see them.
LADY ANNE
Their aunt I am in law, in love their mother:
Then bring me to their sights; I'll bear thy blame
And take thy office from thee, on my peril.
BRAKENBURY
No, madam, no; I may not leave it so:
I am bound by oath, and therefore pardon me.

Exit

Enter LORD STANLEY

LORD STANLEY
Let me but meet you, ladies, one hour hence,
And I'll salute your grace of York as mother,
And reverend looker on, of two fair queens.

To LADY ANNE

Come, madam, you must straight to Westminster,
There to be crowned Richard's royal queen.
QUEEN ELIZABETH
O, cut my lace in sunder, that my pent heart
May have some scope to beat, or else I swoon
With this dead-killing news!

The Tragedy of Richard the Third — Act IV

LADY ANNE
　Despiteful tidings! O unpleasing news!
DORSET
　Be of good cheer: mother, how fares your grace?
QUEEN ELIZABETH
　O Dorset, speak not to me, get thee hence!
　Death and destruction dog thee at the heels;
　Thy mother's name is ominous to children.
　If thou wilt outstrip death, go cross the seas,
　And live with Richmond, from the reach of hell
　Go, hie thee, hie thee from this slaughter-house,
　Lest thou increase the number of the dead;
　And make me die the thrall of Margaret's curse,
　Nor mother, wife, nor England's counted queen.
LORD STANLEY
　Full of wise care is this your counsel, madam.
　Take all the swift advantage of the hours;
　You shall have letters from me to my son
　To meet you on the way, and welcome you.
　Be not ta'en tardy by unwise delay.
DUCHESS OF YORK
　O ill-dispersing wind of misery!
　O my accursed womb, the bed of death!
　A cockatrice hast thou hatch'd to the world,
　Whose unavoided eye is murderous.
LORD STANLEY
　Come, madam, come; I in all haste was sent.
LADY ANNE
　And I in all unwillingness will go.
　I would to God that the inclusive verge
　Of golden metal that must round my brow
　Were red-hot steel, to sear me to the brain!
　Anointed let me be with deadly venom,

   And die, ere men can say, God save the queen!
QUEEN ELIZABETH
   Go, go, poor soul, I envy not thy glory
   To feed my humour, wish thyself no harm.
LADY ANNE
   No! why? When he that is my husband now
   Came to me, as I follow'd Henry's corse,
   When scarce the blood was well wash'd from his hands
   Which issued from my other angel husband
   And that dead saint which then I weeping follow'd;
   O, when, I say, I look'd on Richard's face,
   This was my wish: 'Be thou,' quoth I, ' accursed,
   For making me, so young, so old a widow!
   And, when thou wed'st, let sorrow haunt thy bed;
   And be thy wife--if any be so mad--
   As miserable by the life of thee
   As thou hast made me by my dear lord's death!
   Lo, ere I can repeat this curse again,
   Even in so short a space, my woman's heart
   Grossly grew captive to his honey words
   And proved the subject of my own soul's curse,
   Which ever since hath kept my eyes from rest;
   For never yet one hour in his bed
   Have I enjoy'd the golden dew of sleep,
   But have been waked by his timorous dreams.
   Besides, he hates me for my father Warwick;
   And will, no doubt, shortly be rid of me.
QUEEN ELIZABETH
   Poor heart, adieu! I pity thy complaining.
LADY ANNE
   No more than from my soul I mourn for yours.
QUEEN ELIZABETH
   Farewell, thou woful welcomer of glory!

The Tragedy of Richard the Third — Act IV

LADY ANNE
  Adieu, poor soul, that takest thy leave of it!
DUCHESS OF YORK

  [To DORSET]
  Go thou to Richmond, and good fortune guide thee!

  To LADY ANNE
  Go thou to Richard, and good angels guard thee!

  To QUEEN ELIZABETH
  Go thou to sanctuary, and good thoughts possess thee!
  I to my grave, where peace and rest lie with me!
  Eighty odd years of sorrow have I seen,
  And each hour's joy wrecked with a week of teen.
QUEEN ELIZABETH
  Stay, yet look back with me unto the Tower.
  Pity, you ancient stones, those tender babes
  Whom envy hath immured within your walls!
  Rough cradle for such little pretty ones!
  Rude ragged nurse, old sullen playfellow
  For tender princes, use my babies well!
  So foolish sorrow bids your stones farewell.

Exeunt

SCENE II.
London. The palace.

Sennet. Enter KING RICHARD III, in pomp, crowned; BUCKINGHAM, CATESBY, a page, and others

KING RICHARD III
  Stand all apart Cousin of Buckingham!
BUCKINGHAM
  My gracious sovereign?

KING RICHARD III
  Give me thy hand.

                    Here he ascendeth his throne
  Thus high, by thy advice
  And thy assistance, is King Richard seated;
  But shall we wear these honours for a day?
  Or shall they last, and we rejoice in them?
BUCKINGHAM
  Still live they and for ever may they last!
KING RICHARD III
  O Buckingham, now do I play the touch,
  To try if thou be current gold indeed
  Young Edward lives: think now what I would say.
BUCKINGHAM
  Say on, my loving lord.
KING RICHARD III
  Why, Buckingham, I say, I would be king,
BUCKINGHAM
  Why, so you are, my thrice renowned liege.
KING RICHARD III
  Ha! am I king? 'tis so: but Edward lives.
BUCKINGHAM
  True, noble prince.
KING RICHARD III
  O bitter consequence,
  That Edward still should live! 'True, noble prince!'
  Cousin, thou wert not wont to be so dull:
  Shall I be plain? I wish the bastards dead;
  And I would have it suddenly perform'd.
  What sayest thou? speak suddenly; be brief.
BUCKINGHAM
  Your grace may do your pleasure.
KING RICHARD III
  Tut, tut, thou art all ice, thy kindness freezeth:

The Tragedy of Richard the Third — Act IV

Say, have I thy consent that they shall die?
BUCKINGHAM
Give me some breath, some little pause, my lord
Before I positively herein:
I will resolve your grace immediately.

Exit

CATESBY
[Aside to a stander by]
The king is angry: see, he bites the lip.
KING RICHARD III
I will converse with iron-witted fools
And unrespective boys: none are for me
That look into me with considerate eyes:
High-reaching Buckingham grows circumspect.
Boy!
Page
My lord?
KING RICHARD III
Know'st thou not any whom corrupting gold
Would tempt unto a close exploit of death?
Page
My lord, I know a discontented gentleman,
Whose humble means match not his haughty mind:
Gold were as good as twenty orators,
And will, no doubt, tempt him to any thing.
KING RICHARD III
What is his name?
Page
His name, my lord, is Tyrrel.
KING RICHARD III
I partly know the man: go, call him hither.

Exit Page

The Tragedy of Richard the Third — Act IV

The deep-revolving witty Buckingham
No more shall be the neighbour to my counsel:
Hath he so long held out with me untired,
And stops he now for breath?

Enter STANLEY

How now! what news with you?

STANLEY
My lord, I hear the Marquis Dorset's fled
To Richmond, in those parts beyond the sea
Where he abides.

Stands apart

KING RICHARD III
Catesby!
CATESBY
My lord?
KING RICHARD III
Rumour it abroad
That Anne, my wife, is sick and like to die:
I will take order for her keeping close.
Inquire me out some mean-born gentleman,
Whom I will marry straight to Clarence' daughter:
The boy is foolish, and I fear not him.
Look, how thou dream'st! I say again, give out
That Anne my wife is sick and like to die:
About it; for it stands me much upon,
To stop all hopes whose growth may damage me.

Exit CATESBY

I must be married to my brother's daughter,
Or else my kingdom stands on brittle glass.
Murder her brothers, and then marry her!
Uncertain way of gain! But I am in

The Tragedy of Richard the Third — Act IV

So far in blood that sin will pluck on sin:
Tear-falling pity dwells not in this eye.

Re-enter Page, with TYRREL

Is thy name Tyrrel?
TYRREL
James Tyrrel, and your most obedient subject.
KING RICHARD III
Art thou, indeed?
TYRREL
Prove me, my gracious sovereign.
KING RICHARD III
Darest thou resolve to kill a friend of mine?
TYRREL
Ay, my lord;
But I had rather kill two enemies.
KING RICHARD III
Why, there thou hast it: two deep enemies,
Foes to my rest and my sweet sleep's disturbers
Are they that I would have thee deal upon:
Tyrrel, I mean those bastards in the Tower.
TYRREL
Let me have open means to come to them,
And soon I'll rid you from the fear of them.
KING RICHARD III
Thou sing'st sweet music. Hark, come hither, Tyrrel
Go, by this token: rise, and lend thine ear:

Whispers

There is no more but so: say it is done,
And I will love thee, and prefer thee too.
TYRREL
'Tis done, my gracious lord.
KING RICHARD III
Shall we hear from thee, Tyrrel, ere we sleep?

TYRREL
   Ye shall, my Lord.

Exit

Re-enter BUCKINGHAM

BUCKINGHAM
   My Lord, I have consider'd in my mind
   The late demand that you did sound me in.
KING RICHARD III
   Well, let that pass. Dorset is fled to Richmond.
BUCKINGHAM
   I hear that news, my lord.
KING RICHARD III
   Stanley, he is your wife's son well, look to it.
BUCKINGHAM
   My lord, I claim your gift, my due by promise,
   For which your honour and your faith is pawn'd;
   The earldom of Hereford and the moveables
   The which you promised I should possess.
KING RICHARD III
   Stanley, look to your wife; if she convey
   Letters to Richmond, you shall answer it.
BUCKINGHAM
   What says your highness to my just demand?
KING RICHARD III
   As I remember, Henry the Sixth
   Did prophesy that Richmond should be king,
   When Richmond was a little peevish boy.
   A king, perhaps, perhaps,--
BUCKINGHAM
   My lord!

The Tragedy of Richard the Third — Act IV

KING RICHARD III
  How chance the prophet could not at that time
  Have told me, I being by, that I should kill him?
BUCKINGHAM
  My lord, your promise for the earldom,--
KING RICHARD III
  Richmond! When last I was at Exeter,
  The mayor in courtesy show'd me the castle,
  And call'd it Rougemont: at which name I started,
  Because a bard of Ireland told me once
  I should not live long after I saw Richmond.
BUCKINGHAM
  My Lord!
KING RICHARD III
  Ay, what's o'clock?
BUCKINGHAM
  I am thus bold to put your grace in mind
  Of what you promised me.
KING RICHARD III
  Well, but what's o'clock?
BUCKINGHAM
  Upon the stroke of ten.
KING RICHARD III
  Well, let it strike.
BUCKINGHAM
  Why let it strike?
KING RICHARD III
  Because that, like a Jack, thou keep'st the stroke
  Betwixt thy begging and my meditation.
  I am not in the giving vein to-day.
BUCKINGHAM
  Why, then resolve me whether you will or no.
KING RICHARD III
  Tut, tut,

The Tragedy of Richard the Third — Act IV

Thou troublest me; am not in the vein.

Exeunt all but BUCKINGHAM

BUCKINGHAM
Is it even so? rewards he my true service
With such deep contempt made I him king for this?
O, let me think on Hastings, and be gone
To Brecknock, while my fearful head is on!

Exit

SCENE III.
The same.

Enter TYRREL

TYRREL
The tyrannous and bloody deed is done.
The most arch of piteous massacre
That ever yet this land was guilty of.
Dighton and Forrest, whom I did suborn
To do this ruthless piece of butchery,
Although they were flesh'd villains, bloody dogs,
Melting with tenderness and kind compassion
Wept like two children in their deaths' sad stories.
'Lo, thus' quoth Dighton, 'lay those tender babes:'
'Thus, thus,' quoth Forrest, 'girdling one another
Within their innocent alabaster arms:
Their lips were four red roses on a stalk,
Which in their summer beauty kiss'd each other.
A book of prayers on their pillow lay;
Which once,' quoth Forrest, 'almost changed my mind;
But O! the devil'--there the villain stopp'd
Whilst Dighton thus told on: 'We smothered

The Tragedy of Richard the Third — Act IV

The most replenished sweet work of nature,
That from the prime creation e'er she framed.'
Thus both are gone with conscience and remorse;
They could not speak; and so I left them both,
To bring this tidings to the bloody king.
And here he comes.

Enter KING RICHARD III

All hail, my sovereign liege!

KING RICHARD III
Kind Tyrrel, am I happy in thy news?
TYRREL
If to have done the thing you gave in charge
Beget your happiness, be happy then,
For it is done, my lord.
KING RICHARD III
But didst thou see them dead?
TYRREL
I did, my lord.
KING RICHARD III
And buried, gentle Tyrrel?
TYRREL
The chaplain of the Tower hath buried them;
But how or in what place I do not know.
KING RICHARD III
Come to me, Tyrrel, soon at after supper,
And thou shalt tell the process of their death.
Meantime, but think how I may do thee good,
And be inheritor of thy desire.
Farewell till soon.

Exit TYRREL

The son of Clarence have I pent up close;
His daughter meanly have I match'd in marriage;

The Tragedy of Richard the Third — Act IV

The sons of Edward sleep in Abraham's bosom,
And Anne my wife hath bid the world good night.
Now, for I know the Breton Richmond aims
At young Elizabeth, my brother's daughter,
And, by that knot, looks proudly o'er the crown,
To her I go, a jolly thriving wooer.

Enter CATESBY

CATESBY
My lord!
KING RICHARD III
Good news or bad, that thou comest in so bluntly?
CATESBY
Bad news, my lord: Ely is fled to Richmond;
And Buckingham, back'd with the hardy Welshmen,
Is in the field, and still his power increaseth.
KING RICHARD III
Ely with Richmond troubles me more near
Than Buckingham and his rash-levied army.
Come, I have heard that fearful commenting
Is leaden servitor to dull delay;
Delay leads impotent and snail-paced beggary
Then fiery expedition be my wing,
Jove's Mercury, and herald for a king!
Come, muster men: my counsel is my shield;
We must be brief when traitors brave the field.

Exeunt

SCENE IV.
Before the palace.

Enter QUEEN MARGARET

QUEEN MARGARET
  So, now prosperity begins to mellow
  And drop into the rotten mouth of death.
  Here in these confines slily have I lurk'd,
  To watch the waning of mine adversaries.
  A dire induction am I witness to,
  And will to France, hoping the consequence
  Will prove as bitter, black, and tragical.
  Withdraw thee, wretched Margaret: who comes here?

Enter QUEEN ELIZABETH and the DUCHESS OF YORK

QUEEN ELIZABETH
  Ah, my young princes! ah, my tender babes!
  My unblown flowers, new-appearing sweets!
  If yet your gentle souls fly in the air
  And be not fix'd in doom perpetual,
  Hover about me with your airy wings
  And hear your mother's lamentation!
QUEEN MARGARET
  Hover about her; say, that right for right
  Hath dimm'd your infant morn to aged night.
DUCHESS OF YORK
  So many miseries have crazed my voice,
  That my woe-wearied tongue is mute and dumb,
  Edward Plantagenet, why art thou dead?
QUEEN MARGARET
  Plantagenet doth quit Plantagenet.
  Edward for Edward pays a dying debt.

QUEEN ELIZABETH
　Wilt thou, O God, fly from such gentle lambs,
　And throw them in the entrails of the wolf?
　When didst thou sleep when such a deed was done?
QUEEN MARGARET
　When holy Harry died, and my sweet son.
DUCHESS OF YORK
　Blind sight, dead life, poor mortal living ghost,
　Woe's scene, world's shame, grave's due by life usurp'd,
　Brief abstract and record of tedious days,
　Rest thy unrest on England's lawful earth,

Sitting down

　Unlawfully made drunk with innocents' blood!
QUEEN ELIZABETH
　O, that thou wouldst as well afford a grave
　As thou canst yield a melancholy seat!
　Then would I hide my bones, not rest them here.
　O, who hath any cause to mourn but I?

Sitting down by her

QUEEN MARGARET
　If ancient sorrow be most reverend,
　Give mine the benefit of seniory,
　And let my woes frown on the upper hand.
　If sorrow can admit society,

Sitting down with them

　Tell o'er your woes again by viewing mine:
　I had an Edward, till a Richard kill'd him;
　I had a Harry, till a Richard kill'd him:
　Thou hadst an Edward, till a Richard kill'd him;
　Thou hadst a Richard, till a Richard killed him;
DUCHESS OF YORK
　I had a Richard too, and thou didst kill him;

The Tragedy of Richard the Third — Act IV

    I had a Rutland too, thou holp'st to kill him.
QUEEN MARGARET
    Thou hadst a Clarence too, and Richard kill'd him.
    From forth the kennel of thy womb hath crept
    A hell-hound that doth hunt us all to death:
    That dog, that had his teeth before his eyes,
    To worry lambs and lap their gentle blood,
    That foul defacer of God's handiwork,
    That excellent grand tyrant of the earth,
    That reigns in galled eyes of weeping souls,
    Thy womb let loose, to chase us to our graves.
    O upright, just, and true-disposing God,
    How do I thank thee, that this carnal cur
    Preys on the issue of his mother's body,
    And makes her pew-fellow with others' moan!
DUCHESS OF YORK
    O Harry's wife, triumph not in my woes!
    God witness with me, I have wept for thine.
QUEEN MARGARET
    Bear with me; I am hungry for revenge,
    And now I cloy me with beholding it.
    Thy Edward he is dead, that stabb'd my Edward:
    Thy other Edward dead, to quit my Edward;
    Young York he is but boot, because both they
    Match not the high perfection of my loss:
    Thy Clarence he is dead that kill'd my Edward;
    And the beholders of this tragic play,
    The adulterate Hastings, Rivers, Vaughan, Grey,
    Untimely smother'd in their dusky graves.
    Richard yet lives, hell's black intelligencer,
    Only reserved their factor, to buy souls
    And send them thither: but at hand, at hand,
    Ensues his piteous and unpitied end:
    Earth gapes, hell burns, fiends roar, saints pray.

The Tragedy of Richard the Third — Act IV

    To have him suddenly convey'd away.
    Cancel his bond of life, dear God, I prey,
    That I may live to say, The dog is dead!
QUEEN ELIZABETH
    O, thou didst prophesy the time would come
    That I should wish for thee to help me curse
    That bottled spider, that foul bunch-back'd toad!
QUEEN MARGARET
    I call'd thee then vain flourish of my fortune;
    I call'd thee then poor shadow, painted queen;
    The presentation of but what I was;
    The flattering index of a direful pageant;
    One heaved a-high, to be hurl'd down below;
    A mother only mock'd with two sweet babes;
    A dream of what thou wert, a breath, a bubble,
    A sign of dignity, a garish flag,
    To be the aim of every dangerous shot,
    A queen in jest, only to fill the scene.
    Where is thy husband now? where be thy brothers?
    Where are thy children? wherein dost thou, joy?
    Who sues to thee and cries 'God save the queen'?
    Where be the bending peers that flatter'd thee?
    Where be the thronging troops that follow'd thee?
    Decline all this, and see what now thou art:
    For happy wife, a most distressed widow;
    For joyful mother, one that wails the name;
    For queen, a very caitiff crown'd with care;
    For one being sued to, one that humbly sues;
    For one that scorn'd at me, now scorn'd of me;
    For one being fear'd of all, now fearing one;
    For one commanding all, obey'd of none.
    Thus hath the course of justice wheel'd about,
    And left thee but a very prey to time;
    Having no more but thought of what thou wert,

To torture thee the more, being what thou art.
Thou didst usurp my place, and dost thou not
Usurp the just proportion of my sorrow?
Now thy proud neck bears half my burthen'd yoke;
From which even here I slip my weary neck,
And leave the burthen of it all on thee.
Farewell, York's wife, and queen of sad mischance:
These English woes will make me smile in France.

QUEEN ELIZABETH
O thou well skill'd in curses, stay awhile,
And teach me how to curse mine enemies!

QUEEN MARGARET
Forbear to sleep the nights, and fast the days;
Compare dead happiness with living woe;
Think that thy babes were fairer than they were,
And he that slew them fouler than he is:
Bettering thy loss makes the bad causer worse:
Revolving this will teach thee how to curse.

QUEEN ELIZABETH
My words are dull; O, quicken them with thine!

QUEEN MARGARET
Thy woes will make them sharp, and pierce like mine.

Exit

DUCHESS OF YORK
Why should calamity be full of words?

QUEEN ELIZABETH
Windy attorneys to their client woes,
Airy succeeders of intestate joys,
Poor breathing orators of miseries!
Let them have scope: though what they do impart
Help not all, yet do they ease the heart.

DUCHESS OF YORK
If so, then be not tongue-tied: go with me.

The Tragedy of Richard the Third — Act IV

And in the breath of bitter words let's smother
My damned son, which thy two sweet sons smother'd.
I hear his drum: be copious in exclaims.

Enter KING RICHARD III, marching, with drums and trumpets

KING RICHARD III
Who intercepts my expedition?
DUCHESS OF YORK
O, she that might have intercepted thee,
By strangling thee in her accursed womb
From all the slaughters, wretch, that thou hast done!
QUEEN ELIZABETH
Hidest thou that forehead with a golden crown,
Where should be graven, if that right were right,
The slaughter of the prince that owed that crown,
And the dire death of my two sons and brothers?
Tell me, thou villain slave, where are my children?
DUCHESS OF YORK
Thou toad, thou toad, where is thy brother Clarence?
And little Ned Plantagenet, his son?
QUEEN ELIZABETH
Where is kind Hastings, Rivers, Vaughan, Grey?
KING RICHARD III
A flourish, trumpets! strike alarum, drums!
Let not the heavens hear these tell-tale women
Rail on the Lord's enointed: strike, I say!

Flourish. Alarums

Either be patient, and entreat me fair,
Or with the clamorous report of war
Thus will I drown your exclamations.
DUCHESS OF YORK
Art thou my son?

The Tragedy of Richard the Third — Act IV

KING RICHARD III
  Ay, I thank God, my father, and yourself.
DUCHESS OF YORK
  Then patiently hear my impatience.
KING RICHARD III
  Madam, I have a touch of your condition,
  Which cannot brook the accent of reproof.
DUCHESS OF YORK
  O, let me speak!
KING RICHARD III
  Do then: but I'll not hear.
DUCHESS OF YORK
  I will be mild and gentle in my speech.
KING RICHARD III
  And brief, good mother; for I am in haste.
DUCHESS OF YORK
  Art thou so hasty? I have stay'd for thee,
  God knows, in anguish, pain and agony.
KING RICHARD III
  And came I not at last to comfort you?
DUCHESS OF YORK
  No, by the holy rood, thou know'st it well,
  Thou camest on earth to make the earth my hell.
  A grievous burthen was thy birth to me;
  Tetchy and wayward was thy infancy;
  Thy school-days frightful, desperate, wild, and furious,
  Thy prime of manhood daring, bold, and venturous,
  Thy age confirm'd, proud, subdued, bloody, treacherous,
  More mild, but yet more harmful, kind in hatred:
  What comfortable hour canst thou name,
  That ever graced me in thy company?
KING RICHARD III
  Faith, none, but Humphrey Hour, that call'd

The Tragedy of Richard the Third — Act IV

    your grace
    To breakfast once forth of my company.
    If I be so disgracious in your sight,
    Let me march on, and not offend your grace.
    Strike the drum.
DUCHESS OF YORK
    I prithee, hear me speak.
KING RICHARD III
    You speak too bitterly.
DUCHESS OF YORK
    Hear me a word;
    For I shall never speak to thee again.
KING RICHARD III
    So.
DUCHESS OF YORK
    Either thou wilt die, by God's just ordinance,
    Ere from this war thou turn a conqueror,
    Or I with grief and extreme age shall perish
    And never look upon thy face again.
    Therefore take with thee my most heavy curse;
    Which, in the day of battle, tire thee more
    Than all the complete armour that thou wear'st!
    My prayers on the adverse party fight;
    And there the little souls of Edward's children
    Whisper the spirits of thine enemies
    And promise them success and victory.
    Bloody thou art, bloody will be thy end;
    Shame serves thy life and doth thy death attend.

                              Exit

QUEEN ELIZABETH
    Though far more cause, yet much less spirit to curse
    Abides in me; I say amen to all.

The Tragedy of Richard the Third — Act IV

KING RICHARD III
  Stay, madam; I must speak a word with you.
QUEEN ELIZABETH
  I have no more sons of the royal blood
  For thee to murder: for my daughters, Richard,
  They shall be praying nuns, not weeping queens;
  And therefore level not to hit their lives.
KING RICHARD III
  You have a daughter call'd Elizabeth,
  Virtuous and fair, royal and gracious.
QUEEN ELIZABETH
  And must she die for this? O, let her live,
  And I'll corrupt her manners, stain her beauty;
  Slander myself as false to Edward's bed;
  Throw over her the veil of infamy:
  So she may live unscarr'd of bleeding slaughter,
  I will confess she was not Edward's daughter.
KING RICHARD III
  Wrong not her birth, she is of royal blood.
QUEEN ELIZABETH
  To save her life, I'll say she is not so.
KING RICHARD III
  Her life is only safest in her birth.
QUEEN ELIZABETH
  And only in that safety died her brothers.
KING RICHARD III
  Lo, at their births good stars were opposite.
QUEEN ELIZABETH
  No, to their lives bad friends were contrary.
KING RICHARD III
  All unavoided is the doom of destiny.
QUEEN ELIZABETH
  True, when avoided grace makes destiny:
  My babes were destined to a fairer death,

   If grace had bless'd thee with a fairer life.
KING RICHARD III
   You speak as if that I had slain my cousins.
QUEEN ELIZABETH
   Cousins, indeed; and by their uncle cozen'd
   Of comfort, kingdom, kindred, freedom, life.
   Whose hand soever lanced their tender hearts,
   Thy head, all indirectly, gave direction:
   No doubt the murderous knife was dull and blunt
   Till it was whetted on thy stone-hard heart,
   To revel in the entrails of my lambs.
   But that still use of grief makes wild grief tame,
   My tongue should to thy ears not name my boys
   Till that my nails were anchor'd in thine eyes;
   And I, in such a desperate bay of death,
   Like a poor bark, of sails and tackling reft,
   Rush all to pieces on thy rocky bosom.
KING RICHARD III
   Madam, so thrive I in my enterprise
   And dangerous success of bloody wars,
   As I intend more good to you and yours,
   Than ever you or yours were by me wrong'd!
QUEEN ELIZABETH
   What good is cover'd with the face of heaven,
   To be discover'd, that can do me good?
KING RICHARD III
   The advancement of your children, gentle lady.
QUEEN ELIZABETH
   Up to some scaffold, there to lose their heads?
KING RICHARD III
   No, to the dignity and height of honour
   The high imperial type of this earth's glory.
QUEEN ELIZABETH
   Flatter my sorrows with report of it;

The Tragedy of Richard the Third — Act IV

    Tell me what state, what dignity, what honour,
    Canst thou demise to any child of mine?
KING RICHARD III
    Even all I have; yea, and myself and all,
    Will I withal endow a child of thine;
    So in the Lethe of thy angry soul
    Thou drown the sad remembrance of those wrongs
    Which thou supposest I have done to thee.
QUEEN ELIZABETH
    Be brief, lest that be process of thy kindness
    Last longer telling than thy kindness' date.
KING RICHARD III
    Then know, that from my soul I love thy daughter.
QUEEN ELIZABETH
    My daughter's mother thinks it with her soul.
KING RICHARD III
    What do you think?
QUEEN ELIZABETH
    That thou dost love my daughter from thy soul:
    So from thy soul's love didst thou love her brothers;
    And from my heart's love I do thank thee for it.
KING RICHARD III
    Be not so hasty to confound my meaning:
    I mean, that with my soul I love thy daughter,
    And mean to make her queen of England.
QUEEN ELIZABETH
    Say then, who dost thou mean shall be her king?
KING RICHARD III
    Even he that makes her queen who should be else?
QUEEN ELIZABETH
    What, thou?
KING RICHARD III
    I, even I: what think you of it, madam?

QUEEN ELIZABETH
   How canst thou woo her?
KING RICHARD III
   That would I learn of you,
   As one that are best acquainted with her humour.
QUEEN ELIZABETH
   And wilt thou learn of me?
KING RICHARD III
   Madam, with all my heart.
QUEEN ELIZABETH
   Send to her, by the man that slew her brothers,
   A pair of bleeding-hearts; thereon engrave
   Edward and York; then haply she will weep:
   Therefore present to her--as sometime Margaret
   Did to thy father, steep'd in Rutland's blood,--
   A handkerchief; which, say to her, did drain
   The purple sap from her sweet brother's body
   And bid her dry her weeping eyes therewith.
   If this inducement force her not to love,
   Send her a story of thy noble acts;
   Tell her thou madest away her uncle Clarence,
   Her uncle Rivers; yea, and, for her sake,
   Madest quick conveyance with her good aunt Anne.
KING RICHARD III
   Come, come, you mock me; this is not the way
   To win our daughter.
QUEEN ELIZABETH
   There is no other way
   Unless thou couldst put on some other shape,
   And not be Richard that hath done all this.
KING RICHARD III
   Say that I did all this for love of her.
QUEEN ELIZABETH
   Nay, then indeed she cannot choose but hate thee,

The Tragedy of Richard the Third — Act IV

    Having bought love with such a bloody spoil.
KING RICHARD III
    Look, what is done cannot be now amended:
    Men shall deal unadvisedly sometimes,
    Which after hours give leisure to repent.
    If I did take the kingdom from your sons,
    To make amends, Ill give it to your daughter.
    If I have kill'd the issue of your womb,
    To quicken your increase, I will beget
    Mine issue of your blood upon your daughter
    A grandam's name is little less in love
    Than is the doting title of a mother;
    They are as children but one step below,
    Even of your mettle, of your very blood;
    Of an one pain, save for a night of groans
    Endured of her, for whom you bid like sorrow.
    Your children were vexation to your youth,
    But mine shall be a comfort to your age.
    The loss you have is but a son being king,
    And by that loss your daughter is made queen.
    I cannot make you what amends I would,
    Therefore accept such kindness as I can.
    Dorset your son, that with a fearful soul
    Leads discontented steps in foreign soil,
    This fair alliance quickly shall call home
    To high promotions and great dignity:
    The king, that calls your beauteous daughter wife.
    Familiarly shall call thy Dorset brother;
    Again shall you be mother to a king,
    And all the ruins of distressful times
    Repair'd with double riches of content.
    What! we have many goodly days to see:
    The liquid drops of tears that you have shed
    Shall come again, transform'd to orient pearl,

The Tragedy of Richard the Third — Act IV

    Advantaging their loan with interest
    Of ten times double gain of happiness.
    Go, then my mother, to thy daughter go
    Make bold her bashful years with your experience;
    Prepare her ears to hear a wooer's tale
    Put in her tender heart the aspiring flame
    Of golden sovereignty; acquaint the princess
    With the sweet silent hours of marriage joys
    And when this arm of mine hath chastised
    The petty rebel, dull-brain'd Buckingham,
    Bound with triumphant garlands will I come
    And lead thy daughter to a conqueror's bed;
    To whom I will retail my conquest won,
    And she shall be sole victress, Caesar's Caesar.
QUEEN ELIZABETH
    What were I best to say? her father's brother
    Would be her lord? or shall I say, her uncle?
    Or, he that slew her brothers and her uncles?
    Under what title shall I woo for thee,
    That God, the law, my honour and her love,
    Can make seem pleasing to her tender years?
KING RICHARD III
    Infer fair England's peace by this alliance.
QUEEN ELIZABETH
    Which she shall purchase with still lasting war.
KING RICHARD III
    Say that the king, which may command, entreats.
QUEEN ELIZABETH
    That at her hands which the king's King forbids.
KING RICHARD III
    Say, she shall be a high and mighty queen.
QUEEN ELIZABETH
    To wail the tide, as her mother doth.

The Tragedy of Richard the Third — Act IV

KING RICHARD III
  Say, I will love her everlastingly.
QUEEN ELIZABETH
  But how long shall that title 'ever' last?
KING RICHARD III
  Sweetly in force unto her fair life's end.
QUEEN ELIZABETH
  But how long fairly shall her sweet lie last?
KING RICHARD III
  So long as heaven and nature lengthens it.
QUEEN ELIZABETH
  So long as hell and Richard likes of it.
KING RICHARD III
  Say, I, her sovereign, am her subject love.
QUEEN ELIZABETH
  But she, your subject, loathes such sovereignty.
KING RICHARD III
  Be eloquent in my behalf to her.
QUEEN ELIZABETH
  An honest tale speeds best being plainly told.
KING RICHARD III
  Then in plain terms tell her my loving tale.
QUEEN ELIZABETH
  Plain and not honest is too harsh a style.
KING RICHARD III
  Your reasons are too shallow and too quick.
QUEEN ELIZABETH
  O no, my reasons are too deep and dead;
  Too deep and dead, poor infants, in their grave.
KING RICHARD III
  Harp not on that string, madam; that is past.
QUEEN ELIZABETH
  Harp on it still shall I till heart-strings break.

The Tragedy of Richard the Third — Act IV

KING RICHARD III
  Now, by my George, my garter, and my crown,--
QUEEN ELIZABETH
  Profaned, dishonour'd, and the third usurp'd.
KING RICHARD III
  I swear--
QUEEN ELIZABETH
  By nothing; for this is no oath:
  The George, profaned, hath lost his holy honour;
  The garter, blemish'd, pawn'd his knightly virtue;
  The crown, usurp'd, disgraced his kingly glory.
  if something thou wilt swear to be believed,
  Swear then by something that thou hast not wrong'd.
KING RICHARD III
  Now, by the world--
QUEEN ELIZABETH
  'Tis full of thy foul wrongs.
KING RICHARD III
  My father's death--
QUEEN ELIZABETH
  Thy life hath that dishonour'd.
KING RICHARD III
  Then, by myself--
QUEEN ELIZABETH
  Thyself thyself misusest.
KING RICHARD III
  Why then, by God--
QUEEN ELIZABETH
  God's wrong is most of all.
  If thou hadst fear'd to break an oath by Him,
  The unity the king thy brother made
  Had not been broken, nor my brother slain:
  If thou hadst fear'd to break an oath by Him,
  The imperial metal, circling now thy brow,

The Tragedy of Richard the Third — Act IV

    Had graced the tender temples of my child,
    And both the princes had been breathing here,
    Which now, two tender playfellows to dust,
    Thy broken faith hath made a prey for worms.
    What canst thou swear by now?
KING RICHARD III
    The time to come.
QUEEN ELIZABETH
    That thou hast wronged in the time o'erpast;
    For I myself have many tears to wash
    Hereafter time, for time past wrong'd by thee.
    The children live, whose parents thou hast slaughter'd,
    Ungovern'd youth, to wail it in their age;
    The parents live, whose children thou hast butcher'd,
    Old wither'd plants, to wail it with their age.
    Swear not by time to come; for that thou hast
    Misused ere used, by time misused o'erpast.
KING RICHARD III
    As I intend to prosper and repent,
    So thrive I in my dangerous attempt
    Of hostile arms! myself myself confound!
    Heaven and fortune bar me happy hours!
    Day, yield me not thy light; nor, night, thy rest!
    Be opposite all planets of good luck
    To my proceedings, if, with pure heart's love,
    Immaculate devotion, holy thoughts,
    I tender not thy beauteous princely daughter!
    In her consists my happiness and thine;
    Without her, follows to this land and me,
    To thee, herself, and many a Christian soul,
    Death, desolation, ruin and decay:
    It cannot be avoided but by this;
    It will not be avoided but by this.

The Tragedy of Richard the Third — Act IV

Therefore, good mother,--I must can you so--
Be the attorney of my love to her:
Plead what I will be, not what I have been;
Not my deserts, but what I will deserve:
Urge the necessity and state of times,
And be not peevish-fond in great designs.

QUEEN ELIZABETH
Shall I be tempted of the devil thus?

KING RICHARD III
Ay, if the devil tempt thee to do good.

QUEEN ELIZABETH
Shall I forget myself to be myself?

KING RICHARD III
Ay, if yourself's remembrance wrong yourself.

QUEEN ELIZABETH
But thou didst kill my children.

KING RICHARD III
But in your daughter's womb I bury them:
Where in that nest of spicery they shall breed
Selves of themselves, to your recomforture.

QUEEN ELIZABETH
Shall I go win my daughter to thy will?

KING RICHARD III
And be a happy mother by the deed.

QUEEN ELIZABETH
I go. Write to me very shortly.
And you shall understand from me her mind.

KING RICHARD III
Bear her my true love's kiss; and so, farewell.

Exit QUEEN ELIZABETH

Relenting fool, and shallow, changing woman!

Enter RATCLIFF; CATESBY following

How now! what news?

The Tragedy of Richard the Third — Act IV

RATCLIFF
>My gracious sovereign, on the western coast
>Rideth a puissant navy; to the shore
>Throng many doubtful hollow-hearted friends,
>Unarm'd, and unresolved to beat them back:
>'Tis thought that Richmond is their admiral;
>And there they hull, expecting but the aid
>Of Buckingham to welcome them ashore.

KING RICHARD III
>Some light-foot friend post to the Duke of Norfolk:
>Ratcliff, thyself, or Catesby; where is he?

CATESBY
>Here, my lord.

KING RICHARD III
>Fly to the duke:

To RATCLIFF

>Post thou to Salisbury
>When thou comest thither--

To CATESBY

>Dull, unmindful villain,
>Why stand'st thou still, and go'st not to the duke?

CATESBY
>First, mighty sovereign, let me know your mind,
>What from your grace I shall deliver to him.

KING RICHARD III
>O, true, good Catesby: bid him levy straight
>The greatest strength and power he can make,
>And meet me presently at Salisbury.

CATESBY
>I go.

Exit

RATCLIFF
  What is't your highness' pleasure I shall do at
  Salisbury?
KING RICHARD III
  Why, what wouldst thou do there before I go?
RATCLIFF
  Your highness told me I should post before.
KING RICHARD III
  My mind is changed, sir, my mind is changed.
      Enter STANLEY
  How now, what news with you?
STANLEY
  None good, my lord, to please you with the hearing;
  Nor none so bad, but it may well be told.
KING RICHARD III
  Hoyday, a riddle! neither good nor bad!
  Why dost thou run so many mile about,
  When thou mayst tell thy tale a nearer way?
  Once more, what news?
STANLEY
  Richmond is on the seas.
KING RICHARD III
  There let him sink, and be the seas on him!
  White-liver'd runagate, what doth he there?
STANLEY
  I know not, mighty sovereign, but by guess.
KING RICHARD III
  Well, sir, as you guess, as you guess?
STANLEY
  Stirr'd up by Dorset, Buckingham, and Ely,
  He makes for England, there to claim the crown.
KING RICHARD III
  Is the chair empty? is the sword unsway'd?
  Is the king dead? the empire unpossess'd?

The Tragedy of Richard the Third — Act IV

What heir of York is there alive but we?
And who is England's king but great York's heir?
Then, tell me, what doth he upon the sea?
STANLEY
Unless for that, my liege, I cannot guess.
KING RICHARD III
Unless for that he comes to be your liege,
You cannot guess wherefore the Welshman comes.
Thou wilt revolt, and fly to him, I fear.
STANLEY
No, mighty liege; therefore mistrust me not.
KING RICHARD III
Where is thy power, then, to beat him back?
Where are thy tenants and thy followers?
Are they not now upon the western shore.
Safe-conducting the rebels from their ships!

STANLEY
No, my good lord, my friends are in the north.
KING RICHARD III
Cold friends to Richard: what do they in the north,
When they should serve their sovereign in the west?
STANLEY
They have not been commanded, mighty sovereign:
Please it your majesty to give me leave,
I'll muster up my friends, and meet your grace
Where and what time your majesty shall please.
KING RICHARD III
Ay, ay. thou wouldst be gone to join with Richmond:
I will not trust you, sir.
STANLEY
Most mighty sovereign,
You have no cause to hold my friendship doubtful:
I never was nor never will be false.

KING RICHARD III
   Well,
   Go muster men; but, hear you, leave behind
   Your son, George Stanley: look your faith be firm.
   Or else his head's assurance is but frail.
STANLEY
   So deal with him as I prove true to you.

Exit

Enter a Messenger

Messenger
   My gracious sovereign, now in Devonshire,
   As I by friends am well advertised,
   Sir Edward Courtney, and the haughty prelate
   Bishop of Exeter, his brother there,
   With many more confederates, are in arms.

Enter another Messenger

Second Messenger
   My liege, in Kent the Guildfords are in arms;
   And every hour more competitors
   Flock to their aid, and still their power increaseth.

Enter another Messenger

Third Messenger
   My lord, the army of the Duke of Buckingham--
KING RICHARD III
   Out on you, owls! nothing but songs of death?

He striketh him

   Take that, until thou bring me better news.

The Tragedy of Richard the Third — Act IV

Third Messenger
    The news I have to tell your majesty
    Is, that by sudden floods and fall of waters,
    Buckingham's army is dispersed and scatter'd;
    And he himself wander'd away alone,
    No man knows whither.
KING RICHARD III
    I cry thee mercy:
    There is my purse to cure that blow of thine.
    Hath any well-advised friend proclaim'd
    Reward to him that brings the traitor in?
Third Messenger
    Such proclamation hath been made, my liege.

Enter another Messenger

Fourth Messenger
    Sir Thomas Lovel and Lord Marquis Dorset,
    'Tis said, my liege, in Yorkshire are in arms.
    Yet this good comfort bring I to your grace,
    The Breton navy is dispersed by tempest:
    Richmond, in Yorkshire, sent out a boat
    Unto the shore, to ask those on the banks
    If they were his assistants, yea or no;
    Who answer'd him, they came from Buckingham.
    Upon his party: he, mistrusting them,
    Hoisted sail and made away for Brittany.
KING RICHARD III
    March on, march on, since we are up in arms;
    If not to fight with foreign enemies,
    Yet to beat down these rebels here at home.

Re-enter CATESBY

CATESBY
    My liege, the Duke of Buckingham is taken;

The Tragedy of Richard the Third — Act IV

That is the best news: that the Earl of Richmond
Is with a mighty power landed at Milford,
Is colder tidings, yet they must be told.

KING RICHARD III

Away towards Salisbury! while we reason here,
A royal battle might be won and lost
Some one take order Buckingham be brought
To Salisbury; the rest march on with me.

Flourish. Exeunt

SCENE V.
Lord Derby's house.

Enter DERBY and SIR CHRISTOPHER URSWICK

DERBY

Sir Christopher, tell Richmond this from me:
That in the sty of this most bloody boar
My son George Stanley is frank'd up in hold:
If I revolt, off goes young George's head;
The fear of that withholds my present aid.
But, tell me, where is princely Richmond now?

CHRISTOPHER

At Pembroke, or at Harford-west, in Wales.

DERBY

What men of name resort to him?

CHRISTOPHER

Sir Walter Herbert, a renowned soldier;
Sir Gilbert Talbot, Sir William Stanley;
Oxford, redoubted Pembroke, Sir James Blunt,
And Rice ap Thomas with a valiant crew;
And many more of noble fame and worth:
And towards London they do bend their course,

The Tragedy of Richard the Third — Act IV

    If by the way they be not fought withal.
DERBY
    Return unto thy lord; commend me to him:
    Tell him the queen hath heartily consented
    He shall espouse Elizabeth her daughter.
    These letters will resolve him of my mind. Farewell.

Exeunt

ACT V

SCENE I.
Salisbury. An open place.

Enter the Sheriff, and BUCKINGHAM, with halberds, led to execution

BUCKINGHAM
Will not King Richard let me speak with him?
Sheriff
No, my good lord; therefore be patient.
BUCKINGHAM
Hastings, and Edward's children, Rivers, Grey,
Holy King Henry, and thy fair son Edward,
Vaughan, and all that have miscarried
By underhand corrupted foul injustice,
If that your moody discontented souls
Do through the clouds behold this present hour,
Even for revenge mock my destruction!
This is All-Souls' day, fellows, is it not?
Sheriff
It is, my lord.
BUCKINGHAM
Why, then All-Souls' day is my body's doomsday.
This is the day that, in King Edward's time,
I wish't might fall on me, when I was found
False to his children or his wife's allies
This is the day wherein I wish'd to fall
By the false faith of him I trusted most;
This, this All-Souls' day to my fearful soul
Is the determined respite of my wrongs:
That high All-Seer that I dallied with

The Tragedy of Richard the Third — Act V

Hath turn'd my feigned prayer on my head
And given in earnest what I begg'd in jest.
Thus doth he force the swords of wicked men
To turn their own points on their masters' bosoms:
Now Margaret's curse is fallen upon my head;
'When he,' quoth she, 'shall split thy heart with sorrow,
Remember Margaret was a prophetess.'
Come, sirs, convey me to the block of shame;
Wrong hath but wrong, and blame the due of blame.

Exeunt

SCENE II.
The camp near Tamworth.

Enter RICHMOND, OXFORD, BLUNT, HERBERT, and others, with drum and colours

RICHMOND
   Fellows in arms, and my most loving friends,
   Bruised underneath the yoke of tyranny,
   Thus far into the bowels of the land
   Have we march'd on without impediment;
   And here receive we from our father Stanley
   Lines of fair comfort and encouragement.
   The wretched, bloody, and usurping boar,
   That spoil'd your summer fields and fruitful vines,
   Swills your warm blood like wash, and makes his trough
   In your embowell'd bosoms, this foul swine
   Lies now even in the centre of this isle,
   Near to the town of Leicester, as we learn
   From Tamworth thither is but one day's march.
   In God's name, cheerly on, courageous friends,
   To reap the harvest of perpetual peace

The Tragedy of Richard the Third — Act V

    By this one bloody trial of sharp war.
OXFORD
    Every man's conscience is a thousand swords,
    To fight against that bloody homicide.
HERBERT
    I doubt not but his friends will fly to us.
BLUNT
    He hath no friends but who are friends for fear.
    Which in his greatest need will shrink from him.
RICHMOND
    All for our vantage. Then, in God's name, march:
    True hope is swift, and flies with swallow's wings:
    Kings it makes gods, and meaner creatures kings.

Exeunt

SCENE III.
Bosworth Field.

Enter KING RICHARD III in arms, with NORFOLK, SURREY, and others

KING RICHARD III
    Here pitch our tents, even here in Bosworth field.
    My Lord of Surrey, why look you so sad?
SURREY
    My heart is ten times lighter than my looks.
KING RICHARD III
    My Lord of Norfolk,--
NORFOLK
    Here, most gracious liege.
KING RICHARD III
    Norfolk, we must have knocks; ha! must we not?

The Tragedy of Richard the Third — Act V

NORFOLK
We must both give and take, my gracious lord.
KING RICHARD III
Up with my tent there! here will I lie tonight;
But where to-morrow? Well, all's one for that.
Who hath descried the number of the foe?
NORFOLK
Six or seven thousand is their utmost power.
KING RICHARD III
Why, our battalion trebles that account:
Besides, the king's name is a tower of strength,
Which they upon the adverse party want.
Up with my tent there! Valiant gentlemen,
Let us survey the vantage of the field
Call for some men of sound direction
Let's want no discipline, make no delay,
For, lords, to-morrow is a busy day.

Exeunt

Enter, on the other side of the field, RICHMOND, Sir William Brandon, OXFORD, and others. Some of the Soldiers pitch RICHMOND's tent

RICHMOND
The weary sun hath made a golden set,
And by the bright track of his fiery car,
Gives signal, of a goodly day to-morrow.
Sir William Brandon, you shall bear my standard.
Give me some ink and paper in my tent
I'll draw the form and model of our battle,
Limit each leader to his several charge,
And part in just proportion our small strength.
My Lord of Oxford, you, Sir William Brandon,

The Tragedy of Richard the Third — Act V

And you, Sir Walter Herbert, stay with me.
The Earl of Pembroke keeps his regiment:
Good Captain Blunt, bear my good night to him
And by the second hour in the morning
Desire the earl to see me in my tent:
Yet one thing more, good Blunt, before thou go'st,
Where is Lord Stanley quarter'd, dost thou know?

BLUNT
Unless I have mista'en his colours much,
Which well I am assured I have not done,
His regiment lies half a mile at least
South from the mighty power of the king.

RICHMOND
If without peril it be possible,
Good Captain Blunt, bear my good-night to him,
And give him from me this most needful scroll.

BLUNT
Upon my life, my lord, I'll under-take it;
And so, God give you quiet rest to-night!

RICHMOND
Good night, good Captain Blunt. Come gentlemen,
Let us consult upon to-morrow's business
In to our tent; the air is raw and cold.

They withdraw into the tent

Enter, to his tent, KING RICHARD III, NORFOLK, RATCLIFF, CATESBY, and others

KING RICHARD III
What is't o'clock?

CATESBY
It's supper-time, my lord;
It's nine o'clock.

The Tragedy of Richard the Third — Act V

KING RICHARD III
  I will not sup to-night.
  Give me some ink and paper.
  What, is my beaver easier than it was?
  And all my armour laid into my tent?
CATESBY
  If is, my liege; and all things are in readiness.
KING RICHARD III
  Good Norfolk, hie thee to thy charge;
  Use careful watch, choose trusty sentinels.
NORFOLK
  I go, my lord.
KING RICHARD III
  Stir with the lark to-morrow, gentle Norfolk.
NORFOLK
  I warrant you, my lord.

Exit

KING RICHARD III
  Catesby!
CATESBY
  My lord?
KING RICHARD III
  Send out a pursuivant at arms
  To Stanley's regiment; bid him bring his power
  Before sunrising, lest his son George fall
  Into the blind cave of eternal night.

Exit CATESBY

  Fill me a bowl of wine. Give me a watch.
  Saddle white Surrey for the field to-morrow.
  Look that my staves be sound, and not too heavy.
  Ratcliff!

The Tragedy of Richard the Third — Act V

RATCLIFF
  My lord?
KING RICHARD III
  Saw'st thou the melancholy Lord Northumberland?
RATCLIFF
  Thomas the Earl of Surrey, and himself,
  Much about cock-shut time, from troop to troop
  Went through the army, cheering up the soldiers.
KING RICHARD III
  So, I am satisfied. Give me a bowl of wine:
  I have not that alacrity of spirit,
  Nor cheer of mind, that I was wont to have.
  Set it down. Is ink and paper ready?
RATCLIFF
  It is, my lord.
KING RICHARD III
  Bid my guard watch; leave me.
  Ratcliff, about the mid of night come to my tent
  And help to arm me. Leave me, I say.

Exeunt RATCLIFF and the other Attendants

Enter DERBY to RICHMOND in his tent, Lords and others attending

DERBY
  Fortune and victory sit on thy helm!
RICHMOND
  All comfort that the dark night can afford
  Be to thy person, noble father-in-law!
  Tell me, how fares our loving mother?
DERBY
  I, by attorney, bless thee from thy mother
  Who prays continually for Richmond's good:

The Tragedy of Richard the Third — Act V

    So much for that. The silent hours steal on,
And flaky darkness breaks within the east.
In brief,--for so the season bids us be,--
Prepare thy battle early in the morning,
And put thy fortune to the arbitrement
Of bloody strokes and mortal-staring war.
I, as I may--that which I would I cannot,--
With best advantage will deceive the time,
And aid thee in this doubtful shock of arms:
But on thy side I may not be too forward
Lest, being seen, thy brother, tender George,
Be executed in his father's sight.
Farewell: the leisure and the fearful time
Cuts off the ceremonious vows of love
And ample interchange of sweet discourse,
Which so long sunder'd friends should dwell upon:
God give us leisure for these rites of love!
Once more, adieu: be valiant, and speed well!
RICHMOND
    Good lords, conduct him to his regiment:
I'll strive, with troubled thoughts, to take a nap,
Lest leaden slumber peise me down to-morrow,
When I should mount with wings of victory:
Once more, good night, kind lords and gentlemen.

                Exeunt all but RICHMOND
O Thou, whose captain I account myself,
Look on my forces with a gracious eye;
Put in their hands thy bruising irons of wrath,
That they may crush down with a heavy fall
The usurping helmets of our adversaries!
Make us thy ministers of chastisement,
That we may praise thee in the victory!
To thee I do commend my watchful soul,
Ere I let fall the windows of mine eyes:

The Tragedy of Richard the Third — Act V

Sleeping and waking, O, defend me still!

Sleeps

Enter the Ghost of Prince Edward, son to King Henry VI

Ghost
of Prince Edward
  [To KING RICHARD III]
  Let me sit heavy on thy soul to-morrow!
  Think, how thou stab'dst me in my prime of youth
  At Tewksbury: despair, therefore, and die!
    To RICHMOND
  Be cheerful, Richmond; for the wronged souls
  Of butcher'd princes fight in thy behalf
  King Henry's issue, Richmond, comforts thee.

Enter the Ghost of King Henry VI

Ghost
of King Henry VI
  [To KING RICHARD III]
  When I was mortal, my anointed body
  By thee was punched full of deadly holes
  Think on the Tower and me: despair, and die!
  Harry the Sixth bids thee despair, and die!
    To RICHMOND
  Virtuous and holy, be thou conqueror!
  Harry, that prophesied thou shouldst be king,
  Doth comfort thee in thy sleep: live, and flourish!

Enter the Ghost of CLARENCE

Ghost of CLARENCE
  [To KING RICHARD III]
  Let me sit heavy on thy soul to-morrow!
  I, that was wash'd to death with fulsome wine,

The Tragedy of Richard the Third — Act V

Poor Clarence, by thy guile betrayed to death!
To-morrow in the battle think on me,
And fall thy edgeless sword: despair, and die!--
>*To RICHMOND*

Thou offspring of the house of Lancaster
The wronged heirs of York do pray for thee
Good angels guard thy battle! live, and flourish!

>*Enter the Ghosts of RIVERS, GRAY, and VAUGHAN*

Ghost of RIVERS
>*[To KING RICHARD III]*

Let me sit heavy on thy soul to-morrow,
Rivers. that died at Pomfret! despair, and die!
Ghost of GREY
>*[To KING RICHARD III]*

Think upon Grey, and let thy soul despair!
Ghost of VAUGHAN
>*[To KING RICHARD III]*

Think upon Vaughan, and, with guilty fear,
Let fall thy lance: despair, and die!
All
>*[To RICHMOND]*

Awake, and think our wrongs in Richard's bosom
Will conquer him! awake, and win the day!

>*Enter the Ghost of HASTINGS*

Ghost of HASTINGS
>*[To KING RICHARD III]*

Bloody and guilty, guiltily awake,
And in a bloody battle end thy days!
Think on Lord Hastings: despair, and die!
>*To RICHMOND*

Quiet untroubled soul, awake, awake!

The Tragedy of Richard the Third — Act V

Arm, fight, and conquer, for fair England's sake!

Enter the Ghosts of the two young Princes

Ghosts
of young Princes
    [To KING RICHARD III]
Dream on thy cousins smother'd in the Tower:
Let us be led within thy bosom, Richard,
And weigh thee down to ruin, shame, and death!
Thy nephews' souls bid thee despair and die!
    To RICHMOND
Sleep, Richmond, sleep in peace, and wake in joy;
Good angels guard thee from the boar's annoy!
Live, and beget a happy race of kings!
Edward's unhappy sons do bid thee flourish.

Enter the Ghost of LADY ANNE

Ghost of LADY ANNE
    [To KING RICHARD III]
Richard, thy wife, that wretched Anne thy wife,
That never slept a quiet hour with thee,
Now fills thy sleep with perturbations
To-morrow in the battle think on me,
And fall thy edgeless sword: despair, and die!
    To RICHMOND
Thou quiet soul, sleep thou a quiet sleep
Dream of success and happy victory!
Thy adversary's wife doth pray for thee.

Enter the Ghost of BUCKINGHAM

Ghost
of BUCKINGHAM
    [To KING RICHARD III]
The last was I that helped thee to the crown;

The Tragedy of Richard the Third — Act V

The last was I that felt thy tyranny:
O, in the battle think on Buckingham,
And die in terror of thy guiltiness!
Dream on, dream on, of bloody deeds and death:
Fainting, despair; despairing, yield thy breath!
   To RICHMOND
I died for hope ere I could lend thee aid:
But cheer thy heart, and be thou not dismay'd:
God and good angel fight on Richmond's side;
And Richard falls in height of all his pride.

The Ghosts vanish

KING RICHARD III starts out of his dream

KING RICHARD III
   Give me another horse: bind up my wounds.
   Have mercy, Jesu!--Soft! I did but dream.
   O coward conscience, how dost thou afflict me!
   The lights burn blue. It is now dead midnight.
   Cold fearful drops stand on my trembling flesh.
   What do I fear? myself? there's none else by:
   Richard loves Richard; that is, I am I.
   Is there a murderer here? No. Yes, I am:
   Then fly. What, from myself? Great reason why:
   Lest I revenge. What, myself upon myself?
   Alack. I love myself. Wherefore? for any good
   That I myself have done unto myself?
   O, no! alas, I rather hate myself
   For hateful deeds committed by myself!
   I am a villain: yet I lie. I am not.
   Fool, of thyself speak well: fool, do not flatter.
   My conscience hath a thousand several tongues,
   And every tongue brings in a several tale,

The Tragedy of Richard the Third — Act V

And every tale condemns me for a villain.
Perjury, perjury, in the high'st degree
Murder, stem murder, in the direst degree;
All several sins, all used in each degree,
Throng to the bar, crying all, Guilty! guilty!
I shall despair. There is no creature loves me;
And if I die, no soul shall pity me:
Nay, wherefore should they, since that I myself
Find in myself no pity to myself?
Methought the souls of all that I had murder'd
Came to my tent; and every one did threat
To-morrow's vengeance on the head of Richard.

Enter RATCLIFF

RATCLIFF
  My lord!
KING RICHARD III
  'Zounds! who is there?
RATCLIFF
  Ratcliff, my lord; 'tis I. The early village-cock
  Hath twice done salutation to the morn;
  Your friends are up, and buckle on their armour.
KING RICHARD III
  O Ratcliff, I have dream'd a fearful dream!
  What thinkest thou, will our friends prove all true?
RATCLIFF
  No doubt, my lord.
KING RICHARD III
  O Ratcliff, I fear, I fear,--
RATCLIFF
  Nay, good my lord, be not afraid of shadows.
KING RICHARD III
  By the apostle Paul, shadows to-night
  Have struck more terror to the soul of Richard

The Tragedy of Richard the Third — Act V

Than can the substance of ten thousand soldiers
Armed in proof, and led by shallow Richmond.
It is not yet near day. Come, go with me;
Under our tents I'll play the eaves-dropper,
To see if any mean to shrink from me.

Exeunt

Enter the Lords to RICHMOND, sitting in his tent

LORDS
Good morrow, Richmond!
RICHMOND
Cry mercy, lords and watchful gentlemen,
That you have ta'en a tardy sluggard here.
LORDS
How have you slept, my lord?
RICHMOND
The sweetest sleep, and fairest-boding dreams
That ever enter'd in a drowsy head,
Have I since your departure had, my lords.
Methought their souls, whose bodies Richard murder'd,
Came to my tent, and cried on victory:
I promise you, my soul is very jocund
In the remembrance of so fair a dream.
How far into the morning is it, lords?
LORDS
Upon the stroke of four.
RICHMOND
Why, then 'tis time to arm and give direction.

His oration to his soldiers

More than I have said, loving countrymen,
The leisure and enforcement of the time
Forbids to dwell upon: yet remember this,

The Tragedy of Richard the Third — Act V

God and our good cause fight upon our side;
The prayers of holy saints and wronged souls,
Like high-rear'd bulwarks, stand before our faces;
Richard except, those whom we fight against
Had rather have us win than him they follow:
For what is he they follow? truly, gentlemen,
A bloody tyrant and a homicide;
One raised in blood, and one in blood establish'd;
One that made means to come by what he hath,
And slaughter'd those that were the means to help him;
Abase foul stone, made precious by the foil
Of England's chair, where he is falsely set;
One that hath ever been God's enemy:
Then, if you fight against God's enemy,
God will in justice ward you as his soldiers;
If you do sweat to put a tyrant down,
You sleep in peace, the tyrant being slain;
If you do fight against your country's foes,
Your country's fat shall pay your pains the hire;
If you do fight in safeguard of your wives,
Your wives shall welcome home the conquerors;
If you do free your children from the sword,
Your children's children quit it in your age.
Then, in the name of God and all these rights,
Advance your standards, draw your willing swords.
For me, the ransom of my bold attempt
Shall be this cold corpse on the earth's cold face;
But if I thrive, the gain of my attempt
The least of you shall share his part thereof.
Sound drums and trumpets boldly and cheerfully;
God and Saint George! Richmond and victory!

Exeunt

The Tragedy of Richard the Third — Act V

Re-enter KING RICHARD, RATCLIFF, Attendants and Forces

KING RICHARD III
   What said Northumberland as touching Richmond?
RATCLIFF
   That he was never trained up in arms.
KING RICHARD III
   He said the truth: and what said Surrey then?
RATCLIFF
   He smiled and said 'The better for our purpose.'
KING RICHARD III
   He was in the right; and so indeed it is.

Clock striketh

   Ten the clock there. Give me a calendar.
   Who saw the sun to-day?

RATCLIFF
   Not I, my lord.
KING RICHARD III
   Then he disdains to shine; for by the book
   He should have braved the east an hour ago
   A black day will it be to somebody. Ratcliff!
RATCLIFF
   My lord?
KING RICHARD III
   The sun will not be seen to-day;
   The sky doth frown and lour upon our army.
   I would these dewy tears were from the ground.
   Not shine to-day! Why, what is that to me
   More than to Richmond? for the selfsame heaven
   That frowns on me looks sadly upon him.

Enter NORFOLK

The Tragedy of Richard the Third — Act V

NORFOLK
  Arm, arm, my lord; the foe vaunts in the field.
KING RICHARD III
  Come, bustle, bustle; caparison my horse.
  Call up Lord Stanley, bid him bring his power:
  I will lead forth my soldiers to the plain,
  And thus my battle shall be ordered:
  My foreward shall be drawn out all in length,
  Consisting equally of horse and foot;
  Our archers shall be placed in the midst
  John Duke of Norfolk, Thomas Earl of Surrey,
  Shall have the leading of this foot and horse.
  They thus directed, we will follow
  In the main battle, whose puissance on either side
  Shall be well winged with our chiefest horse.
  This, and Saint George to boot! What think'st thou, Norfolk?
NORFOLK
  A good direction, warlike sovereign.
  This found I on my tent this morning.

He sheweth him a paper

KING RICHARD III
  [Reads]
  'Jockey of Norfolk, be not too bold,
  For Dickon thy master is bought and sold.'
  A thing devised by the enemy.
  Go, gentleman, every man unto his charge
  Let not our babbling dreams affright our souls:
  Conscience is but a word that cowards use,
  Devised at first to keep the strong in awe:
  Our strong arms be our conscience, swords our law.
  March on, join bravely, let us to't pell-mell
  If not to heaven, then hand in hand to hell.

The Tragedy of Richard the Third — Act V

His oration to his Army
What shall I say more than I have inferr'd?
Remember whom you are to cope withal;
A sort of vagabonds, rascals, and runaways,
A scum of Bretons, and base lackey peasants,
Whom their o'er-cloyed country vomits forth
To desperate ventures and assured destruction.
You sleeping safe, they bring to you unrest;
You having lands, and blest with beauteous wives,
They would restrain the one, distain the other.
And who doth lead them but a paltry fellow,
Long kept in Bretagne at our mother's cost?
A milk-sop, one that never in his life
Felt so much cold as over shoes in snow?
Let's whip these stragglers o'er the seas again;
Lash hence these overweening rags of France,
These famish'd beggars, weary of their lives;
Who, but for dreaming on this fond exploit,
For want of means, poor rats, had hang'd themselves:
If we be conquer'd, let men conquer us,
And not these bastard Bretons; whom our fathers
Have in their own land beaten, bobb'd, and thump'd,
And in record, left them the heirs of shame.
Shall these enjoy our lands? lie with our wives?
Ravish our daughters?

Drum afar off

Hark! I hear their drum.
Fight, gentlemen of England! fight, bold yoemen!
Draw, archers, draw your arrows to the head!
Spur your proud horses hard, and ride in blood;
Amaze the welkin with your broken staves!

Enter a Messenger

What says Lord Stanley? will he bring his power?

Messenger
   My lord, he doth deny to come.
KING RICHARD III
   Off with his son George's head!
NORFOLK
   My lord, the enemy is past the marsh
   After the battle let George Stanley die.
KING RICHARD III
   A thousand hearts are great within my bosom:
   Advance our standards, set upon our foes
   Our ancient word of courage, fair Saint George,
   Inspire us with the spleen of fiery dragons!
   Upon them! victory sits on our helms.

Exeunt

SCENE IV.
Another part of the field.

Alarum: excursions. Enter NORFOLK and forces fighting; to him CATESBY

CATESBY
   Rescue, my Lord of Norfolk, rescue, rescue!
   The king enacts more wonders than a man,
   Daring an opposite to every danger:
   His horse is slain, and all on foot he fights,
   Seeking for Richmond in the throat of death.
   Rescue, fair lord, or else the day is lost!

   Alarums. Enter KING RICHARD III

KING RICHARD III
   A horse! a horse! my kingdom for a horse!

The Tragedy of Richard the Third — Act V

CATESBY
  Withdraw, my lord; I'll help you to a horse.
KING RICHARD III
  Slave, I have set my life upon a cast,
  And I will stand the hazard of the die:
  I think there be six Richmonds in the field;
  Five have I slain to-day instead of him.
  A horse! a horse! my kingdom for a horse!

Exeunt

SCENE V.
Another part of the field.

Alarum. Enter KING RICHARD III and RICHMOND; they fight. KING RICHARD III is slain. Retreat and flourish. Re-enter RICHMOND, DERBY bearing the crown, with divers other Lords

RICHMOND
  God and your arms be praised, victorious friends,
  The day is ours, the bloody dog is dead.
DERBY
  Courageous Richmond, well hast thou acquit thee.
  Lo, here, this long-usurped royalty
  From the dead temples of this bloody wretch
  Have I pluck'd off, to grace thy brows withal:
  Wear it, enjoy it, and make much of it.
RICHMOND
  Great God of heaven, say Amen to all!
  But, tell me, is young George Stanley living?
DERBY
  He is, my lord, and safe in Leicester town;
  Whither, if it please you, we may now withdraw us.
RICHMOND
  What men of name are slain on either side?

The Tragedy of Richard the Third — Act V

DERBY
  John Duke of Norfolk, Walter Lord Ferrers,
  Sir Robert Brakenbury, and Sir William Brandon.
RICHMOND
  Inter their bodies as becomes their births:
  Proclaim a pardon to the soldiers fled
  That in submission will return to us:
  And then, as we have ta'en the sacrament,
  We will unite the white rose and the red:
  Smile heaven upon this fair conjunction,
  That long have frown'd upon their enmity!
  What traitor hears me, and says not amen?
  England hath long been mad, and scarr'd herself;
  The brother blindly shed the brother's blood,
  The father rashly slaughter'd his own son,
  The son, compell'd, been butcher to the sire:
  All this divided York and Lancaster,
  Divided in their dire division,
  O, now, let Richmond and Elizabeth,
  The true succeeders of each royal house,
  By God's fair ordinance conjoin together!
  And let their heirs, God, if thy will be so.
  Enrich the time to come with smooth-faced peace,
  With smiling plenty and fair prosperous days!
  Abate the edge of traitors, gracious Lord,
  That would reduce these bloody days again,
  And make poor England weep in streams of blood!
  Let them not live to taste this land's increase
  That would with treason wound this fair land's peace!
  Now civil wounds are stopp'd, peace lives again:
  That she may long live here, God say amen!

Exeunt

Hedingham Castle
The Birthplace of Edward de Vere

The manor of Hedingham was awarded to Aubrey de Vere I by William the Conqueror sometime before 1086. The castle was constructed by the de Veres in the late 11th and early 12th centuries, and the Keep (shown) in the 1130s and 1140s. It is the only part of the castle that has survived. The castle was held by the de Vere family until 1625.

Today, the castle is the residence of the Lindsay family, direct descendants of the de Veres, but it is also used as a striking venue for educational tours and other public and private events. Short of a personal visit, it's possible to take the most captivating '3D Virtual Tour' at the Hedingham Castle website:
> https://www.hedinghamcastle.co.uk/visit
> (Scroll down to find the tour.)

Biography

A Short Life of Edward de Vere, 17th Earl of Oxford

by Dr. Kevin Gilvary, President
The de Vere Society

He was born on 12 April 1550 at Castle Hedingham, his family's ancestral home. His father, John de Vere, 16th Earl, was Lord Great Chamberlain and attended the coronations of both Mary and Elizabeth Tudor. His mother was Margaret Golding. Edward was 11 when, in 1561, Queen Elizabeth visited Hedingham for four days of masques, feasting and entertainments. When his father died in 1562, young Oxford left to become, like Bertram in *All's Well that Ends Well*, a ward of the Crown under the guardianship of William Cecil, the Queen's private secretary (later Lord Burghley, Lord Treasurer). His mother married Charles Tyrrell and seems to have passed out of the boy's life. His sister Mary went to live with her stepfather and the siblings were not reunited for some years.

    According to a curriculum in Cecil's own hand, Edward de Vere's daily studies included dancing, French, Latin, writing and drawing, cosmography, penmanship, riding, shooting, exercise and prayer. Edward de Vere showed a prodigious talent for scholarship from his early years, and we may ascribe his lifelong love of learning to the influence of two of his early tutors. The first was Sir Thomas Smith who was, perhaps, England's most respected Greek scholar and the former Cambridge tutor of Sir William Cecil. It was, no doubt, through Cecil's influence that Edward de Vere spent some time living in the household of Smith in his early years, during which time he spent about five months at Smith's alma mater, Queens' College, Cambridge. Smith was a scholar of widely varied interests – this was reflected in his 400-volume library, some of which is still extant at Cambridge. De Vere's other tutor was Laurence Nowell, who was not only an accomplished cartographer but was also England's premier scholar of Anglo-Saxon literature – it was Nowell who possessed the only known copy of *Beowulf*.

Another important influence on Edward de Vere's early studies was his maternal uncle Arthur Golding, an officer in the Court of Wards under Cecil, who is credited with the translation of Ovid's *Metamorphoses*, published in 1567, a book widely recognised as having a major influence on 'Shakespeare'.

Following on from his matriculation at Cambridge in November 1558, Edward was awarded an honorary MA by Cambridge during a Royal progress in August 1564, and another degree by Oxford University during a Royal progress in 1566. Edward de Vere then attended Gray's Inn to study law. One notable feature of the Elizabethan Inns of Court was a tradition of mounting dramatic productions and of hosting the various touring companies of players.

In 1570 he served in a military campaign in Scotland under the Earl of Sussex. By 1571, he was reported as a leading luminary of the Court and, for a time, a favourite of Queen Elizabeth. In December 1571 he married Anne Cecil, aged 15, daughter of his guardian. This was a dynastic marriage where all the advantage accrued to Cecil who, ennobled as Baron Burghley, had reduced the social gap between himself and the young Earl.

While Oxford was away on a Grand Tour of Europe, he heard that his daughter Elizabeth Vere had been born in July 1575. On his return in early 1576, he appeared to have been convinced that Elizabeth was not his child; consequently he became estranged from Anne for five years, and exiled himself from Court, taking up residence in the Savoy and concerning himself with literary and musical patronage.

Already, in 1573, *Cardanus Comfort* (the Consolations of Boethius) had been translated from Latin by Thomas Bedingfield and dedicated to Oxford; and published with a preface written by him. In 1576 an anthology, *A Paradise of Daintie Devices*, including several poems by Oxford, was published. These are juvenile works but already show affinities, in both style and thought, with those of the mature Shakespeare.

Oxford's Grand Tour had taken in Paris, Strasbourg, Venice, Genoa, Florence, Palermo and, on his way back through France, Rousillon – the setting for *Love's Labour's Lost*. Oxford spent the best part of a year travelling in Italy in 1576, and becoming involved with moneylenders. He came back to England fluent in Italian and well acquainted with the northern Italian cities, to be satirised by Gabriel Harvey as 'The Italian Earl'. On his way back his ship was attacked by pirates in the English Channel (cf. *Hamlet*). Fourteen of 'Shakespeare's' plays have Italian settings, in which he put his detailed knowledge of the country, beyond pure book knowledge, to good use.

1573 saw the birth of Henry Wriothesley, Earl of Southampton. Although history has not bequeathed to us any evidence of a direct relationship between the two men, in the relatively small world of the royal Court, they must have been acquainted with each other. The poems *Venus and Adonis* (1593) and *The Rape of Lucrece* (1594) were dedicated to Southampton. These were the first works to be published under the name 'Shakespeare' and for the next five years the records show the byline 'Shakespeare' to have been associated exclusively with these two poems. Plays under the name 'Shakespeare' did not appear in print until 1598, the year that Lord Burghley died.

In May 1577 Oxford invested in Frobisher's voyage in the ship *Edward Bonaventure*. Despite its name, the ship's voyage across the Atlantic in search of the North-West Passage lost money; consequently he was forced to sell three estates (cf. Hamlet's words 'I am but mad north-north-west' II.1.). In 1578 he invested in Frobisher's second expedition, which also lost money, forcing further sales of estates.

He was mentioned by Gabriel Harvey in an address to Queen Elizabeth in July 1578, as a prolific private poet and one 'whose countenance shakes spears'. In the same year John Lyly, Oxford's secretary, published *Euphues.The Anatomy of Wit*, followed in 1579 by *Euphues and his England*, dedicated to Oxford. These two books launched the fashion for 'Euphuism', a style characterized by high-flown language, satirized in *Love's Labour's Lost*.

In March 1581 Oxford's mistress, Anne Vavasour, who was one of Queen Elizabeth's Ladies of the Bedchamber, gave birth to a son. The lovers and their son were sent to the Tower by an infuriated Queen but swiftly released (cf. *Measure for Measure*). After his release, Oxford was wounded in a street-fight provoked by Thomas Knyvet, a kinsman of Anne Vavasour; affrays continued in the streets of London between the rival gangs of supporters for over a year (cf.*Romeo and Juliet*).

In December 1581 he resumed living with his long-suffering and devoted wife, and accepted Elizabeth

Vere as his child. Tragically, their only son died one day after his birth. Three more daughters followed, of whom Susan and Bridget survived.

In 1584, Robert Greene's *Gwydonius; the Card of Fancy* was dedicated to him, identifying him as a 'pre-eminent writer'. In 1586, when he was 36, he served on the tribunal which condemned Mary, Queen of Scots to execution.

In the same year, the Queen awarded Oxford an unconditional pension of £1,000 a year for life (about £500,000 at today's value). The motive for this uncharacteristic generosity on the part of the Queen remains a mystery – no accounting was required of Oxford. Her successor, King James I, continued to pay the pension. In reply to Sir Robert Cecil's request that Lord Sheffield's pension be increased, the King refused, saying, 'Great Oxford got no more . . .', leaving us to wonder why Great Oxford? His greatness does not seem to have resided in war or any of the known offices of State. Perhaps a clue can be found in a letter to Burghley, written in 1594, in which Edward de Vere seeks his favour in a matter involving what he describes as 'in mine office' and that this office is beholden to the Queen.

In 1589, George Puttenham published *The Arte of English Poesie* and this contains the most telling recognition of Edward de Vere's literary standing amongst his contemporaries: 'And in her Majesties time that now is are sprong up an other crew of Courtly makers Noble men and Gentlemen of her Majesties owne servantes, who have written excellently well as it would appear if their doings could be found out and made publicke with the rest, of which number is first that noble Gentleman Edward Earle of Oxford.'

In 1588 his wife Anne, daughter of Lord Burghley, died and in extant letters written at this time, it is reported that Burghley is so incapacitated by grief over the death of his favourite daughter that he is incapable of conducting any Privy Council business.

Three years later, in 1591, Oxford married another of the Queen's Maids of Honour, Elizabeth Trentham, with whom he finally became the father of a male heir; Henry de Vere, 18th Earl of Oxford. Although there is evidence of his continued involvement in Court affairs, from the date of this marriage Edward de Vere's life at his new home at King's Place in Hackney is perhaps the most obscure of his entire life.

In 1594, his ship the *Edward Bonaventure* was wrecked in Bermuda (cf. *The Tempest*). In January 1595, Elizabeth Vere married William Stanley, 6th Earl of Derby, another literary earl who maintained his own company of players – many scholars believe that *A Midsummer Night's Dream* was written for these festivities which were attended by the whole royal Court.

On September 7 1598, Francis Meres' *Palladis Tamia* was registered for publication, naming Oxford as the 'best for comedy'. This is a vital document in Shakespearean history because it includes the first mention of 'Shakespeare' as a playwright, attributing twelve plays to him; until then Shakespeare's reputation had rested on the two narrative poems only.

Oxford suffered all his life from financial difficulties, much of which can be traced to the fact that Queen Elizabeth handed out the bulk of his estate to her favourite courtier the Earl of Leicester during Oxford's minority as a royal ward (estates which Oxford found almost impossible to reclaim), and the ruinous debt she placed upon him over his marriage to Anne Cecil. It is, however, notable that his new brother-in-law, the wealthy Staffordshire landowner and Knight of the Shire Francis Trentham, took over the management of Edward de

Vere's near-bankrupt estate from 1591 and gradually nursed it back to health so that, when Oxford died, all of his massive debts had been cleared.

On the Queen's death in 1603 Oxford wrote eloquently to Sir Robert Cecil, son and heir of Lord Burghley, of his 'great grief'. He wrote, 'In this common shipwreck, mine is above all the rest, who least regarded, though often comforted, she hath left to try my fortune among the alterations of time and chance'.

Oxford died in Hackney in 1604, cause unknown. Parish records state that he was buried in Hackney Church on July 6, but a family history by his first cousin Percival Golding, states 'Edward de Veer ... a man in mind and body absolutely accomplished with honorable endowments ... lieth buried at Westminster'. No record of such a burial can now be traced in Westminster Abbey, where there is a Vere family tomb.

The Aftermath of Oxford's life and death

During the winter season 1604-05, six of Shakespeare's plays were presented at Court by command of King James I. This has an air of commemoration. In 1609 the *Sonnets* were published in a pirated edition. The famous dedication describes the author as 'our ever-living', a phrase invariably used only of the dead.

In 1622 Henry Peacham published, in *The Compleat Gentelman*, a list of poets who made Elizabeth's reign a 'golden age'. Unaccountably, he omitted Shakespeare but placed the Earl of Oxford in first place in his list – perhaps he knew them to be the same person. This is unlike Meres who included them both – maybe one reason was because he didn't know Oxford and Shakespeare were the same person.

We do not know who instigated publication of the First Folio Edition of the Shakespeare plays in 1623, but there is no mention of any executor or relative of Shakspere of Stratford in connection with it. However, of the two brothers who financed it and to whom it was dedicated, one – Philip Earl of Montgomery – was the husband of Oxford's daughter Susan, while the other – William Earl of Pembroke – had once been a suitor for her sister Bridget. Pembroke was Lord Chamberlain, the supreme authority in the world of theatre, and thus in a position to decide which plays were to be published and which suppressed. We also know that Ben Jonson, who wrote much of the introductory material, was an intimate associate of the de Vere family after Oxford's death. The First Folio was therefore very much a family affair, but the family was not the one in Stratford-on-Avon.

Coat of Arms of Edward de Vere, 17th Earl of Oxford

Vero Nihil Verius
Nothing is Truer than [de] Vere [Truth]

This is the coat of arms that was fashioned for [by] Edward himself in 1574 and published in the medical book of the de Vere family physician, George Baker, entitled *Oleum Magistrale*. This dedication of his book to Edward de Vere on the part of Dr. Baker is thought to be in recognition of Edward's expertise in the medical sciences as well as in the traditions of heraldry that are so much in evidence throughout his plays and poetry.

An AfterVerse

*For those with yet an interest
In strenuous debate
We've compiled a list of books and films
Your appetite to sate.
From this study clear your mind
Of doubt and all misgiving-
Who from us has long since gone
And who is ever-living.*

Selected References & Bibliography
About the Author
Edward de Vere, 17th Earl of Oxford

Books

♦ Anderson, M. (2005). *Shakespeare by Another Name: The Life of Edward de Vere, Earl of Oxford, The Man who was Shakespeare.* New York: Gotham Books.
--*A physicist by training with research interest in how evidence supports or negates a theory, Mark Anderson spent ten years investigating Edward de Vere as the author of Shake-speare's works.*

♦Farina, William. (2006). *De Vere as Shakespeare: An Oxfordian Reading of the Canon.* Jefferson, NC. McFarland & Company.

--Each of the plays and poems is individually assessed and explored in its own chapter, using the innumerable connections between the text itself and the life of its author, Edward de Vere.

♦ Looney, J. Thomas (2018). *Shakespeare Identified.* Cary, N.C. Veritas Publicaations.
--First published in 1920 this book began the modern Oxfordian movement. From reading it, Sigmund Freud became convinced and John Galsworthy called it "the best detective story I ever read."

♦ Ogburn, C. (1992). *The Mysterious William Shakespeare.* McLean (Va.): EPM.
--An in depth exploration and must read foundational book on the authorship question.

♦Sobran, Joseph. (1997). *Alias Shakespeare: Solving the Greatest Literary Mystery of All Time.* New York; The Free Press, A Division of Simon & Schuster.
--A concise exploration of the puzzling questions surrounding the authorship controversy with the evidence decisively supporting the case for Edward de Vere, the 17th Earl of Oxford, as the rightful author of the Shakespeare plays and poems.

♦Whittemore, Hank. (2016), *100 Reasons Shake-speare Was the Earl of Oxford.* Somerville MA. Forever Press.
▶ Also with further discussion and public comment at: *Hank Whittemore's Shakespeare Blog.*
          https://hankwhittemore.com/
--In both the book and online blog cited above, Whittemore presents a concise introduction to the

authority question that examines 100 different aspects, from biographical and historical records, that point to Edward de Vere as the true writer of the Shake-speare plays and poems.

Websites & Videos

▶ De Vere Society. (2019). The de Vere Society – Dedicated to the proposition that the works of Shakespeare were written by Edward de Vere, 17th Earl of Oxford. [online] Deveresociety.co.uk. Available at: https://deveresociety.co.uk
--A very complete resource with substantial biographical and authorship information and links.

▶ The Oxford Fellowship (2019). Shakespeare Oxford Fellowship | Research and Discussion of the Shakespeare Authorship Question. [online] Shakespeare Oxford Fellowship. Available at: https://shakespeareoxfordfellowship.org/
--A seminal online resource especially focusing on the authorship question.

▶ Waugh, A. (2019). Alexander Waugh. [online] YouTube. Available at: https://www.youtube.com/channel/UCHN7SCKlsa9lPYJmqqQ2uIg/featured/
OR simply search: 'Alexander Waugh'
--Alexander Waugh is a leading authorship scholar who has produced many fascinating video presentations on the authorship question. This link is to his YouTube Channel.

▶ Columbia Pictures & Centropolis Entertainment. (2011). *Anonymous*. Produced and directed by Roland Emmerich. [DVD]
--This mainstream film is both entertaining and enlightening. It presents a superb dramatization of the character of Edward de Vere, setting out in detail the historical and personal context which made his anonymous authorship necessary.

▶Centropolis Entertainment and First Folio Pictures. *Last Will and Testament.* (2012). [DVD]
--A thoughtful and ground-breaking video documentary introduction to the Shakespeare authorship question.

Acknowledgment
Our sincere thanks to
The de Vere Society
and
The Shakespeare Oxford Fellowship
*for their inspiration, help and support
in creating this series.*

Attributions
*--Character list from Wikipedia under
the Creative Commons License 3.0
--Play text from the Moby(tm) editions
in the public domain*

Photos
Coat of Arms of Edward de Vere
Source: Wikimedia.org
Author: George Baker / Public domain

The Keep at Castle Hedingham
Source: geograph.org.uk
Author: David Phillips / CC BY-SA 2.0

Cover inset: Image from a portrait of Richard III of England (1520). Held by The Society of Antiquaries, London.

Cover/Inside: The Welbeck portrait of Edward de Vere (1575). Artist unknown. National Portrait Gallery, London.

This work has been edited and produced by

Verus Publishing
www.verusbooks.com

www.ingramcontent.com/pod-product-compliance
Lightning Source LLC
Chambersburg PA
CBHW031629160426

43196CB00006B/343